I0762859

The Beauty of Being
WEIRD

The Beauty of Being WEIRD

A Psychologist's Guide to Living Guilt-Free

DR. SERGI RUFI

Translated by Dustin Langan

HANOVER
SQUARE
PRESS

ISBN-13: 978-1-335-00133-7

The Beauty of Being Weird

Translated by Dustin Langan

Hanover Square Press
22 Adelaide St. West, 41st Floor
Toronto, Ontario M5H 4E3, Canada
HanoverSqPress.com

HarperCollins Publishers
Macken House, 39/40 Mayor Street Upper,
Dublin 1, D01 C9W8, Ireland
www.HarperCollins.com

Printed in U.S.A.

This book was inspired while traveling on the road.
I dedicate it to Víctor, my mirror of beauty
and my source of inspiration.

Everything Is Topsy-Turvy

People tell me that I'm different,
That I swim against the current.
They tell me that I'll never change,
Another loser at this game.

When you believe all that you see,
Everything is topsy-turvy.
What they say that you witness
Is solely in their interest.

They say no one understands me,
That alone no one can beat me.
They say I'm not immortal
And I'll surely burn in Hell.

When you believe all that you see,
Everything is topsy-turvy.
What they say that you witness
Is solely in their interest.

The weird ones challenge norms!
Old questions in new forms!
Shake the dust from the worn veil!
The old Empire won't prevail!

Contents

Author's Note

When the ubiquitous space between cosmic consciousness and psychological time vanishes, human possibilities multiply infinitely. That is when we become divine beings.

The idea above may sound beautiful and hopeful, but it really doesn't say anything specific, let alone anything practical or useful. Once it fades from memory, it will have no therapeutic effect on anyone.

I've used this New Age, Disneyfied rhetoric to captivate readers and make them feel like I possess a higher degree of understanding of "ultimate reality." This way, they'll think that everything I say deserves to be heard and taken into consideration.

However, I actually don't claim to know everything, and I'm not trying to sell anything to anyone. I also don't intend to set a high bar that could frustrate anyone or make them need to come back to me for another hit.

I'm not a mainstream psychologist, a know-it-all or some fake enlightened guru. Most books on psychology and spirituality are full of good intentions, but that is not enough to truly and honestly understand who we are.

I will only talk about my personal and professional

experience gained over more than twenty-five years of involvement in psychology and spirituality, supporting thousands of people from many different cultures and countries.

I believe that books on psychology should be written by rigorous psychologists, not economists, businesspeople, journalists or engineers. Otherwise, we'll end up thinking that the mind is as precise as a mathematical formula or a linear equation: a one-way street with no turning back.

And we'll fall into the trap of thinking that if this other person could do it, then we can too. We'll believe there is a single, foolproof method for everyone and mistake someone else's story for our own path to growth.

Ultimately, I hope to fall short of your expectations. I hope you've knocked me off that pedestal by the time you've finished the book.

I'm no braver than anyone else. I'm simply myself, and I share what thoughts and ideas I can.

Invitation to the Beauty of Being Weird

We are living in a strange time of complexity and contrast, of *replication* and *evolution*, of change and acceptance, of guilt and freedom, of values and anti-values,[1] of narcissism and shyness, of noise and silence, of curiosity and boredom, of comfort and disorder, of appearance and feeling, of hyperconnectivity and solitude, of firmness and gentleness, of façade and sensitivity, of **weirdness** and **beauty**.

We can capitalize on today's **cultural confusion** to open ourselves to our **human contradictions** and better **understand** ourselves. Or we can close our eyes and let this opportunity for transformation slip away forever, missing the chance to live as our true selves, **lighter and with less guilt**.

---

1 Anti-values are behaviors or beliefs that oppose or undermine humanistic values, such as selfishness, envy, covetousness and greed.

Introduction

The ideas I explore in this book are based on over twenty-five years of experience in the field of psychology, first as a student, then as a professional psychologist. During this long journey, I have met, analyzed and supported thousands of people in their personal development all over the world.

Just as textbooks on particle physics are written by physicists and building design manuals are written by architects, psychology textbooks should be written by psychologists experienced in therapeutic intervention and support. You don't become a cardiologist just because you have a heart or a mechanic just because you have a car.

However, merely for having a mind, having overcome a crisis or having achieved financial success, many people follow trends and start to preach axioms about psychology or push fail-safe methods for **controlling** the mind and supposedly living a **happier** life. This is how psychology has become the area of human knowledge most overrun with unqualified practitioners, where anyone can present their **truth** as fact to stand out in the field.

Businesspeople, economists, entrepreneurs, engineers, journalists and bankers all write bestsellers about psychology, generalizing from their personal experience, projecting their example onto society and leaving people more confused than ever.

This is how popular psychology, the type that sells the most and is the most widespread, has ended up claiming that we are all the same, that we all follow the same patterns and that we therefore all need the same solutions. Its view of the human condition is reductionist, simplistic, superficial, linear . . . and therefore harmful.

This dime-store psychology is no match for the rigor of therapeutic practice. Its mistaken conclusions are debunked by directly engaging with the deepest layers of thousands of people.

I am convinced that any psychology book or method that adds more tension, rigidity, manufactured fear, guilt or shame, rather than offering real solutions to personal struggles, just ends up creating a new problem to tackle. I believe that if our nervous system detects a general therapeutic recommendation as threatening, we should reject it. Our parents, teachers and bosses have already shouted at us enough.

The purpose of this book is for readers to gain a deeper understanding of themselves, including their thoughts, emotions and behaviors, so they can manage their lives more effectively, change what they can about themselves and accept more gracefully what they cannot. It aims to help them live with less **guilt** and **shame** about who they are and whatever they may be going through, find more **meaning** in their lives and connect with and express a more authentic and **real** self while embracing their own personal **weirdness**, with all their quirks and peculiarities.

The questions I'm asked most frequently in my practice are, "Is what's happening to me **normal**?", "Do I have a serious problem?" and "Am I crazy?" People's **confusion** about their experience comes from that superficial and shortsighted approach to psychology that I mentioned above. What is truly crazy is forcing what is **different** to be normal.

IT'S TIME TO FREE OURSELVES FROM FEELING GUILTY FOR NOT FITTING INTO WHAT MAINSTREAM CULTURE CASTS AS NORMAL.

When you stumble upon a **concept** that fits you to a T, your eyes light up, a shiver runs up your spine, your heart beats faster and you feel convinced. The pieces of your mental puzzle fall into place. You feel a connection when you recognize yourself in a serious textbook. It seems like someone is talking about you, and you feel less alone.

Some internal traits and processes can trigger feelings

of **weirdness** within, such as high sensitivity, neurodivergence, introversion, giftedness, branching thinking, lateral thinking, divergent thinking and so on.

Other key concepts are essential for understanding ourselves better, such as homeokinesis (a dynamic and changing internal equilibrium), psychological variability, multifactoriality, complexity, understanding, compassion, sensitivity, uncertainty, beauty, acceptance, values, freedom, guilt, humility and *Homo insipiens*.

Throughout the book, I use some similar and almost interchangeable terms that refer to the nervous system, such as the *lower pathway* (or bottom-up), the ascending pathway, the somatic level, feeling, sensing, the unconscious mind, the unconscious, intuition, instinct, sensitivity, automatism, the mammal and the inner primate. My personal nervous system is Serginess, which is found in me alone and often determines important aspects of my way of being and my decision-making.

I also mention the *higher pathway* (or top-down), the descending pathway or the rational part, which tries to control the nervous system, and the *upper pathway*, which encompasses values, principles and spirituality.

Furthermore, when I talk about **mainstream culture**, I am specifically referring to the "religion of science" (or dogmatic scientism), academic psychology (the cognitive-behavioral paradigm): a New Age, Disneyfied doctrine (simplistic magical-positive thinking), traditional (monistic) religion, commercial media and social media culture (narcissistic histrionics or hypertransparency). In general, I am referring to all one-dimensional, mainstream thinking that flows from powerful organizations and the ways they wield power, all for their exclusive gain.

I feel a philosophical, psychological and spiritual affinity with Hayes's Acceptance and Commitment Therapy (ACT), Porges's Polyvagal Theory, Assagioli's psychosynthesis and Piero Ferrucci's books, the Neo-Advaita tradition, Wayne Liquorman's books, as well as Alfonso López Quintás's Creative Intelligence Methodology.

I am deeply grateful to all my artistic **influences** for their contribution and inspiration in clarifying human behavior, helping me understand life better and freeing me from the extra baggage of guilt and shame with which mainstream culture burdens us from the moment we are born.

Evolution

Evolution requires elimination.
Erykah Badu

My weirdness was probably recognizable from the dawn of my existence. My first few days in my mother's womb must not have been easy. I was most likely a strange zygote. The trend didn't change once my body passed through my mother's birth canal and I first experienced the open air.

As a baby, I was clearly cognitively, emotionally and behaviorally different from my brother, who was thirteen months older than me. As a child, teenager, young adult and adult, these differences only multiplied. My brother turned out to be a good, docile and *replicative* son. I became a bad, rebellious and *evolutive* son.

Nobody in my family suggested any possible **reasons** for my obvious weirdness. It was up to me to discover the causes of my behavior that set me apart from the rest of the family, which I did through my own research and my professional training as a psychologist. My grandmother, with a vacant stare and tears in her eyes, recalled that when my mother was pregnant with my brother, she was her **normal** self: cheerful, talkative and lively. However, when she was pregnant with me, she seemed **strange**, sad and downcast.

When I was born, my mother was clinically depressed. She separated from my father, returned to her parents' house—my grandparents—and left me in the care of her six brothers and sisters. However, her depression only got worse. Those were different times. No one knew anything about psychology or the world of emotions. Deep conversations were rare, and even showing emotion or **fragility** in public was frowned upon.

My mother was the eldest daughter, a role model who received everyone's devotion. She was her parents' favorite child, her siblings' favorite sister, her friends' favorite friend and the most productive worker in her company. "She was the smartest, the friendliest and the most beautiful," her inner circle told me again and again when I was a young man searching for answers.

She saw several psychiatrists during her illness, underwent various treatments and was treated with different drugs. She eventually stopped eating, ceased talking completely and attempted suicide several times. Her large family and friends poured their hearts into her. She was hospitalized for a while, but she never regained her **natural** state of mind.

One morning, when I was nine months old, she

left home and never returned. She was missing for two weeks while her family, friends, acquaintances and the police searched for her. Finally, Linda, the family dog, discovered her lifeless body on the roof of the building where my grandparents lived. During all that time, she had been so close, yet so far away.

My brother and I lived with my mother's family for over two years. We had lost our mother, and her family was devastated. However, we had four aunts and a grandmother who tried to fill our mother's role, nurturing us with security, protection, attention and affection. This part of my family is emotionally close-knit. Individually, they are kind, helpful, devoted, permissive and respectful people.

I experienced my second **trauma** when I was just over two years old. One summer afternoon, my father came to get me and my brother, and we moved permanently into his house with his new wife (my stepmother). Overnight, we went from living in a kind, warm and calm family environment to one that felt repressive, cold and tense.

It makes sense that around that time, with so many open emotional wounds, I began to behave somewhat strangely compared to other children my age. In preschool, teachers noticed the **difference** between my strong abilities and my poor attitude, saying things like, "He abuses trust," "He abuses power" and "He distracts the class."

At that time, psychology was just beginning to take shape in Spain. It was considered a second-class field of knowledge.

Just as my mother died from a lack of knowledge, **understanding** and communication, as well as from excessive shame and guilt, I set out on my journey at a time when the inner world was a forbidden place, feelings were fairy tales, psychological depth was a symptom of imbalance, and the only validated form of emotional management was repression and silence.

It's important to know our **starting** point and recognize the baseline from which we begin our lives. It used to be denied, but today, neuroscience confirms that a pregnant woman's mental health directly impacts the mental health of the fetus, just as parenting later affects the child's psychological development.

I probably developed in cold and **unsafe** amniotic fluid. Maybe the placenta didn't provide me with enough of the necessary, quality nutrients. Maybe the umbilical cord that connected me to my mother was somewhat weak and fragmented.

Evolution

We are the result of perinatal conditions, a type of maternal attachment, a parenting style and the emotional atmosphere at **home**. We are children born into a particular family situation, with genetic and environmental conditions that we did not choose willingly or rationally, and with which we must deal for the rest of our lives. They are birthmarks and birth wounds.

Since I was a child of cortisol, it was natural that I cried more at night, that I was more rebellious, that I easily became overwhelmed, that I demanded more attention, that I fought more, that I was rough and that I had a lot of energy. The winds of the past blow the **storms** of today.

I was an impulsive child. I acted without thinking and felt without words. My gut was always two steps ahead of my thoughts. I was born of tragedy, and my childhood and adolescence were filled with strain and intensity.[1]

Thank God I have been able to dedicate the last twenty-five years to psychology—first as a student, then as a university professor and researcher, and finally as an individual and group psychotherapist. During all this time, I have worked psychologically, emotionally and spiritually with thousands of people from many different countries and cultures.

---

1 For more details, you can read *Una psicología real.*

I have concluded that very few of us come from truly structured families with parent–child relationships rooted in **secure attachments**. My story is no more dramatic than that of at least fifty percent of the world's population. I only know a few people who had totally happy childhoods. There are many myths around the subject, a lot of romanticization and a great deal of silence and secrecy. So many façades and fairy tales are presented to us that don't have anything to do with everyday reality.

If we cover up or turn a blind eye to the **causes** and conditions that shaped us, we will mistake them for the consequences and blame ourselves for the state we're in today.

The truth lies deep beneath the surface, and to slowly let go of the guilt and shame we have inherited, we must practice a kind of **biographical spelunking**. Though its roots are invisible, just like the past, it is essential that we understand the quality of the soil where the **seed** of our tree was planted. We also need to be aware of the climate and the environment in which it grew, grasping the type and quality of its branches, leaves and fruit.

Considering the parents we've had, with their limited emotional education, extreme personalities, unhealed **traumas**, unresolved conflicts and disorders and addictions, who raised us without the proper tools and resources to help us grow healthily, we can be thankful for the miracle of being alive.

All the things that we did not choose are what shaped our nervous system, our immune system and all the other systems crucial for our physical and psychological survival. Instead of being rocked in a cradle, it's as if we grew up in the trenches. To be fair, we're doing pretty well after all that we've been through. Figuratively speaking, there are not enough parents and too many children.

Our mind–body organism has an unconscious part and a conscious part.

Consciously, I can say that I am Sergi Rufi. I can learn about and **understand myself** better through personal observation and direct experience, as well as through comparison to others and information I receive from people. However, observing, knowing and understanding myself is not the same as choosing, **deciding** and acting intentionally.

I can feel my heartbeat, the rhythm of my breathing and a sudden pang in my gut. I can smell my armpits and taste my tongue at any given moment. However, I cannot make my heart beat the way I want it to, control my breathing rate all the time, stop my digestive system from hurting whenever I want or change my body odor at any time with the power of a single thought.

There is also another deep and unconscious part: an ancestral brain that governs the neurophysiological processes of my mind–body organism. This deep part controls my physical, emotional and cognitive metabolism. Most of our biological processes are **autonomous** and independent of our reasoning, as are most of our thoughts, emotions and mental images. They emerge and fade automatically in the background of our attention. Sergi Rufi can do little to stop these processes' unconscious ebb and flow.

This set of unconscious and automatic systems (the central and peripheral nervous systems [sympathetic and parasympathetic]), the immune system, the endocrine system and so on is what I call **Serginess**. I am aware that Sergi Rufi (my conscious part) has not willingly and rationally chosen Serginess. Instead, Sergi Rufi is a reflection of the genetically and environmentally conditioned responses of Serginess, which precedes him, since it began to form nine months before Sergi Rufi officially arrived on the scene on May 29.

I understand the impact that **Victorianess**, the unconscious part of my mother (Victoria), had on Serginess during my gestation and the first few months of my life until her death and subsequent absence.

Furthermore, after I was born, positive and negative interactions with my caregivers, their different attachment and parenting styles, family traumas, school, teachers and my first classmates and friends also had a direct influence on how Serginess learned to respond to pleasant and unpleasant situations in the environment.

In other words, I, Sergi Rufi, am an unchosen outcome of **Rufism**—the virtues and limitations, traditions and traumas of my mother's family, Rufi—and of **Canism**—the virtues and limitations, traditions and traumas of my father's family, Cano. It is important for Sergi Rufi to know as much as possible about Serginess, including how it grew, where it comes from, what it has been through and where it's broken. It is essential for him to understand that most of the punishment, rejection and humiliation he has experienced were due to the unconscious tendencies of Serginess.

He must know that human beings, and especially the most **sensitive** among us, live their lives from the bottom up and that nobody has ever consciously decided on their temperament, inclinations and preferences. Everything emanated from the unconscious part, which we could not mold to our liking. It is the result of many elements of which we may have some clue, but most of which we don't know in detail.

It is important for Sergi Rufi to know as much as possible about Serginess, to try to change what he can and accept what he can't. He must make peace with it, act tenderly toward it and stop struggling against the inevitable. He must learn to move with the wind and not against it. He must want to be who he is and not push back against his instincts and intuition.

Serginess is what decides when I put on a sweater because I'm cold, when I go to bed because I'm sleepy, when I ponder something and when I don't, when I go for a walk and when I lie down on the couch.

LIFE CAN'T TURN OUT TOO POORLY FOR US IF WE LIVE CONNECTED TO OUR INSTINCTS, FEELINGS, INTUITION AND PRINCIPLES.

This is true even if we must **free ourselves** from guilt and learn things all over again.

Academic psychology, which draws on mathematics and rationalist philosophy, promotes the idea of free will, which is inherited from conventional religion. And it blames our natural—and automatic—way of being for being different. They want us to be insensitive, fearful and superficial followers. And they have shamed us for not fitting the mainstream **mold**.

Therefore, Sergi Rufi is a reflection of Serginess, and not the other way around. Sergi Rufi is not to blame for the **conditions** of his birth and upbringing that make him the way he is. Sergi Rufi takes responsibility for the consequences of his actions when they affect others, but he doesn't feel guilty for being the way he is.

Just as I don't feel guilty about being unable to synthesize a digestive enzyme since that process is a part of my biology, I don't feel guilty about my temperament, character and personality either. I know myself, I **understand** myself, I try to change what I can and I accept what I cannot. With this more precise and precious way of experiencing myself, I have shed tons of guilt and shame. I **allow** myself to feel what I feel, opening myself to life and to inner experiences. I have given up on trying to be someone I never was and never will be.

Finally, as time goes on, I'm increasingly experiencing the original **unity** of body and mind. Sergi Rufi is merely a consequence, and he is gradually becoming more at ease with **Serginess**.

There are four ways to live your life:

- Mode 1: Family fusion.[2] We feel deeply connected to the family home, living in peace, security and harmony with our family. We stick closely to the rules and fulfill the expectations

2 Just as you can be in fusion with your emotions (see page 15, below), you can be in fusion or enmeshed with your family. In this sense, your individual boundaries are blurred, and you confuse yourself, your tastes, your opinions and your desires with those of your family members.

of the family to which we belong. We naturally adopt its inclinations, politics, tastes, preferences and traditions. We are an extension of the family, another cog in its machine.

- Mode 2: Family shame and guilt. We follow our family's rules and meet its expectations, even though we feel a certain conflict of interest. Deep down, we feel limited, incomplete and frustrated. We sense that we are living half-heartedly and feel compelled, with an underlying feeling of emptiness, incompleteness and pointless inertia.
- Mode 3: Individual shame and guilt. We have moved away from our family's rules and expectations, living separate from the family and following the beat of our own drum, though we pay the price with feelings of resentment, guilt and personal inadequacy. We feel resistance from our family as we follow our path; being the black sheep of the family or the odd man out is a lot to bear.
- Mode 4: Individual path. We live apart from our family. We have won autonomy and agency through our own movement, walking our personal path with meaning and conviction. We have distanced ourselves from our family, though we are not separated from it, and we are on a rewarding journey of growth, discovery and learning.

Kant said that we don't see things as they are, but we see them as we are. Personally, I believe we don't see things as we are, but *as we are at each given moment*. Since we are alive and therefore dynamic, we are in constant internal motion.

We all experience, interpret and decide things based on our **emotional states**. We will view life in one way or another based on how we feel at any particular time. If I feel joyful, I will also feel more capable, inspired and connected. If I feel sad, tired or frustrated, I will also feel more incapable and detached from people and from the **rhythm** of life.

We can differentiate the intensity of these internal states with three basic colors: red, yellow and green.

- **Red** represents a very high level of intensity, which includes emotional fusion, hyperactivation, somatization, overflow, dysregulation and an acute sense of threat and concern about a specific situation.
- **Yellow** represents a state of medium intensity, where we perceive a certain emotional detachment from the situation. Though we are uncomfortable, we experience this sensation more dynamically than in the red state. This intensity level is more manageable.

- **Green** represents an internal state of calm, regulation and comfortable detachment from events. In the green state, we have regained our center, with full perspective, and can analyze events with more levelheadedness.

We could further subdivide this scale and make it more useful and tailored to our daily experience. It could be more realistic to distinguish five colors that range from the highest to the lowest emotional intensity experienced: red, red–yellow, yellow, yellow–green and green.

At one extreme, red would represent the most distressing expression of any unpleasant emotion, be it sadness, anger, fear, guilt, shame, frustration and helplessness. Green would represent calmness, tranquility, security, comfort, a sense of emotional release and satiety.

It is quicker and easier to connect with **colors** to understand our inner state. They also help us explain our inner state and share it with others. Colors, symbols and images are more effective than other means of description because it can be hard to find the right words when we're emotionally activated.

Furthermore, by naming colors, we avoid hyperobservation and hyperanalysis, which tend to build psychological tension. Complex descriptions can lead to overthinking and rumination, which increase emotional fusion[3] and intensify psychological discomfort.

It is important to let go of the idea that if life isn't "green," it means you're doing something wrong. If you are sensitive, reflective and honest, your inner **traffic light** will constantly be changing. Life isn't always smooth sailing.

We might find ourselves in the green state when we're lying down, resting, disconnected from digital devices or engaging in activities that make us feel fully reconnected, fulfilled and rested. This often happens close to nature or animals, or while savoring life's simple pleasures. However, life is generally **yellow**, with all its attendant tension, challenges, fears, resistance and obstacles.

Red is a difficult state to navigate for long. However, nothing can protect us from hardship and guarantee that we stay in the green light. Not even living isolated in nature, on a desert island, with our lover or lying in a hammock can ensure that. Living together, interacting, the very design of human life, the wiring of our brain and the unconscious responses of the nervous system all compel us to move constantly through our internal traffic light.

---

3 Emotional fusion (more commonly known as cognitive fusion, though it can also involve emotions) refers to a phenomenon in which a person becomes entangled with their thoughts or emotions to the point that they experience them as absolute truths, rather than as transient mental events.

There are no traffic lights with just one color, just as nobody can live in the same state forever.

Finally, we could say three things. A life worth living includes a certain amount of risk and calmness and is therefore **yellow**. A yellow–green state should be a realistic and attainable natural state for all. Red should be a state of temporary alarm, where we should not remain for too long and from which we should be able to calmly emerge. To achieve this, we need to know and understand ourselves better so we can put ourselves in situations that naturally help our nervous system to perform at its best.

There are two basic tendencies when relating to the world: replicating it or evolving within it.

Replicative people are those who tend to replicate and preserve automatic psychosocial patterns and behaviors. They are well adapted to mainstream culture and conventional life. They show a general tendency toward **conformity** with the norm, and follow traditional standards and nonreflective rationality. *Replicative* people are mirrors that repeat mainstream imagery and reproduce the world. They are closed off to novelty, do not worry and follow set and unchanging routines. They live in apparent order, with the rigor of cognitive repetition and security. For *replicative* people, there are good guys and bad guys, heroes and villains.

Evolutive people tend to challenge and reevaluate automatic psychosocial patterns and behaviors. They are uncomfortable with the mainstream mold and standard ways of life. They generally lean toward curiosity, **questioning** the norm and embracing emotional intensity. They are more critical, introspective and less predictable. *Evolutive* people are both sponges and hammers: they are drawn to **novelty** and change. For *evolutive* people, the concepts of good and bad are relative and shaped by perspective, values and mood. Both extremes of good and evil are found in the same person.

Both types of people are necessary to maintain a healthy civilization. Neither is better or more important than the other. We could speculate that around eighty percent of the world's population is *replicative* and the remaining twenty percent is *evolutive*. And the problem lies in that difference.

We all harbor **impulses** within us. Each is a living *movement* activated over time, depending on the environment in which we find ourselves (at work, with family, with friends, with our partner and so on) and the *moment* of each person's life (childhood, adolescence, youth, adulthood and old age).

We can view both **tendencies** as invisible lenses

through which we perceive and interpret reality, forming the basis for our action. Both lenses differ in their degree of depth, sensitivity and awareness.

A *replicative* person works with dolphins in aquariums, feeding, petting and training them to perform the best tricks in shows. In contrast, the *evolutive* dolphin lover frees them from captivity so they can return to their home, the ocean. Both consider themselves dolphin lovers.

A *replicative* person works in the arms industry, believing that military technology helps defend the country and maintain world order. An *evolutive* person refuses to support the arms industry because it starts wars and sows death and misery. Both believe in peace and human dignity.

It is a matter of perspective and the angle from which issues are analyzed and how deeply life is lived.

Finally, **replicative** people live life in a **set** way according to modes 1 or 2 (as depicted on pages 11–12), whereas **evolutive** people experience all four modes of life as *changing phases*, moving from mode 1 to 4 throughout life as part of a natural and organic transformation.

It is important to remember that no one rationally and willingly chooses their natural tendency or the way they live their life. Differences **occur** spontaneously in the interaction between our genetic influences and what we learn from our surroundings.

In general, our level of understanding doesn't depend on any conscious decision. You don't have to flip a switch to turn on the light bulb. Our own perspective broadens on its own, when the time comes. To some, this happens in the cradle, and to others, on the way to the grave.

Control

It's easier to fool someone
than to convince them that
they have been fooled.

Commonly attributed to Mark Twain

The word change generates excitement, motivation and hope. Advertisers are well-versed in its suggestive power, and politicians are proficient in leveraging its persuasive strength. In the campaign for the last municipal elections in Spain, the following slogans appeared below the photos of the main candidates: "Vote for change," "The change you deserve," "The change you need" and "Real change." Regardless of their political platform, they all used the same propagandistic phrase, even though essentially nothing changed.

The word *change* is a magic concept, as the philosopher Alfonso López Quintás would say. It is sold as an elixir for all ills, a solution to all problems. The idea of being able to change something at will has attracted, enticed, motivated, fascinated and enchanted human beings since the dawn of time.

The same thing happens in psychology and spirituality. I started meditating in 2005 after reading an interview with a long-time meditator who claimed that meditating twice a day for twenty minutes had profoundly changed his personality. And who is satisfied with the way they are? Who hasn't been made to feel ashamed for how they see the world or live within it? Who doesn't want to expand their horizons and rein in their excesses? Who isn't drawn to the promise of a balanced, calm and equanimous life? Indeed, meditation and yoga are sold as another panacea, another cure-all, to the point that people who practice them assume a kind of moral superiority over those who don't.

The **promise** of widespread, constant and long-term sustainable **change** is a captivating advertising gimmick. The drive for internal change drags half of humanity along, inspiring grandiose fantasies in the collective unconscious. These expectations are toxic because we will never truly fulfill them; there will always be a gap between what I am and what I would like to be. It is an ideal, a romantic notion that is not realistically attainable. **Change** is the goose that lays the golden eggs of advertising, the carrot that leads the donkey along. It is what gets us moving and makes us constantly strive to transform ourselves, to modify ourselves and to keep the flame of incessant growth burning.

They sell the exception as the rule. What if it happened to me? What if I won the lottery? What if I became enlightened? It's the same principle used in gambling, which leads to compulsive behavior and addiction. The same as Bitcoin, with promises of easy money and living happily ever after.

It is true that we do have some flexibility and can change certain physical and material aspects of ourselves. For example, we can reshape our eyebrows and lengthen our eyelashes, alter our skin tone with makeup, dye our hair, lose or gain weight, tone our bodies, change our height with heels and transform our appearance with tattoos. We can change our car, house, job and partner. Psychologically, however, it's not so simple. Our way of being is a reflection of our nervous system and various biological systems (such as our endocrine, immune and digestive systems), which have been influenced by many different past genetic and environmental factors, both from our previous experiences and from the lessons we've learned. And these factors continue to be influenced by many ongoing phenomena.

In other words, no matter how hard I try, I, Sergi Rufi, cannot mold **Serginess** to my liking. We don't yet have implants or microchips to control and alter our vital functions at will. We still aren't cyborgs. Instead, we have a mold that defines our potential and limitations: a heightened way of being that almost "lives us." It is also true that we will change throughout our lives (it's an inevitable part of existence) and that if we do the right psychological work, we can let go of deep-seated tensions, process unexplored emotions, heal chronic grief and overcome past traumas. There is room for transformation in how we feel. There are some things that we can change and others that we simply cannot.

A proton can't have a negative electric charge, and gravity can't pull us upward. Fish can't fly, and cats can't bark. Plum trees can't produce almonds. Likewise, we can't make a television wash clothes like a washing machine or make flowers grow from the face of a stone.

In the same way, each of us is different and has a limited number of functions that we can perform optimally. We have a certain range of aptitudes and talents to develop. We also have certain limitations. Each of us has particular tendencies and inclinations, but not others.

No matter how much exercise, dietary changes, belief systems or meditation techniques we employ; no matter how much mainstream culture pressures us to change our appearance, our way of being and our very soul—in the long run, we will only succeed in running ourselves ragged. It is pointless to struggle against the laws of physics, chemistry and human biology.

Nevertheless, countless gurus use the same advertising techniques as politicians. They sell books, hold workshops and give talks under the glittering promise of

reinvention. They urge radical change to eradicate those underlying feelings of mediocrity and boredom forever.

Personally, after working with thousands of clients, I don't know anyone who has reinvented themselves. Many have sloughed off old emotional burdens, learned to tread more gently in the present and opened themselves to continuous evolution.

Professionally, I've met a handful of people who have changed radically. I know an engineer who left the office to work in the fields and an economist who swapped Excel for the paintbrush and canvas.

However, I believe that the idea of reinvention as a three-hundred-sixty-degree psychological revolution, a before and after, a clean slate—as some people advocate—is actually a poisoned chalice. It's an illusion presented to us like a breath of fresh air, like a beautiful utopia, like a sweet dream that quickly turns into a dystopian nightmare, from which we wake up in a cold sweat.

And the worst part is the bitter aftertaste left behind. We end up saying, "I could do more" and "I should achieve more," indicating that "everyone seems to be able do it except me" and that "if they can do it but I can't, there's something wrong with me." Once again, over time, the lure of advertising ends in more helplessness, frustration and guilt.

The virus of self-sufficiency is everywhere. To appear respectable is commendable, but to always appear flawless is contemptible.

In downtown Barcelona, there is a well-known man with a physical deformity that has left him without legs. The man believes that he carries himself with dignity because he doesn't beg for money. Instead, he spreads out a blanket to display small wooden elephants he carves himself. When you give him a coin, he hands you a wooden elephant. If you tell him that you don't need it, he gets offended and upset.

He believes in an equal exchange between peers, not in helping others. Cases like his are extreme, and it's certainly admirable that people with such severe challenges know how to maintain a sense of equity. Those who were supposed to care for such people surely caused them great harm. They don't trust others, their kindness or their honesty.

The problem is that in most cases, this display of self-sufficiency, of being emotionally closed off, of not needing anything, is a form of posturing that only makes loneliness and helplessness worse.

WE NEED TO LEARN TO ASK FOR HELP AND TO LET PEOPLE HELP US. WE NEED TO CONNECT WITH SENSITIVITY AND WITH OUR WOUNDS, THEN UNITE WITH THE REST OF HUMANITY.

We must learn to trust others more and let people give us support. All disorders arise from a sense of separation. Our nervous system needs to connect with others' nervous systems. It needs to mend broken bonds, foster intimacy, get in tune with others and find comfort in the assurance that we won't be hurt again.

Some people are born into privilege and don't know how to ask for or receive help. Nothing can be given to them without them feeling ashamed of their failure because they had to "depend" on others.

To feel secure, mentally healthy, confident and open to experience, we must maintain a certain sense of internal and external **control**. We need to have a sense that we can manage what we feel and think and that we can solve problems as they come up.

To a certain extent, it is healthy to sustain the illusion that I (and only I), Sergi Rufi, am the captain of my ship, that I (and only I) am the one steering Serginess. However, if I am humbler and more exacting in my analysis, I must acknowledge that my personal successes and failures depend more on Serginess than on myself. In fact, this is much truer than Sergi Rufi would like to admit.

In other words, my path and destiny, whether straight or winding, depend more on what is autonomous and unconscious within me, "that which lies within"

(Serginess), which precedes and underlies my rational consciousness and will (Sergi Rufi), as well as on the situations that life presents to me. A simple fact is worth more than a thousand thoughts.

The truth is that the direction that my life takes is related to my decisions and actions, which are directly connected to my IQ, my emotional state and my ability to manage my emotions, my level of self-awareness, my attitudes and my limitations. And I don't remember having consciously chosen any of that. It also depends on the time and context in which I operate.

I can be an expert in civil engineering, be fluent in several languages, and have over a decade of experience working with top companies in the United States, the United Kingdom and Australia, and still fail to make the cut in the first interview for a job that fits me like a glove.

However, that result doesn't invalidate the previous assessment. It's simply incomplete, as it doesn't consider many other uncontrollable and unknown factors that could influence the outcome. For example, I may have reminded the interviewer of her ex, so she didn't like me. There might have been more qualified candidates and even less qualified candidates who better matched the company's philosophy.

Mainstream science loves to spread the idea that it has a monopoly on the truth. It claims that its diagnoses, treatments and prognoses, based on theories, hypotheses, remedies and conclusions, are infallible. And if the prediction fails, it's not due to any mistake in the approach or the prescribed method, but rather it's the individual's fault. Mainstream science never apologizes.

Likewise, we all tend to overlook some of our failures to avoid the harsh truth that we can only really feel like we have a tiny bit of control over the present and even less over the future. A young and happy father can die of a stroke. An athlete favored to win a tournament can twist his ankle. A bride who seems deeply in love can leave the groom standing at the altar. A CEO can flop when addressing the foundation's annual meeting and get demoted to manager.

Furthermore, we may think about doing something, and even want to do it, but never follow through. We can imagine that we'd never do something and suddenly end up doing it. We can despise someone, then later become their good friend. We can wish for something with all our might and never accomplish it.

We can achieve something without deserving it. We can deserve it, then achieve it. We can decide to never do something again and end up doing it again.

Our nervous system is an indecipherable machine that not only influences our thoughts, emotions and behaviors, but also produces and directs them. It is a universe shaped by many different variables. It is often unpredictable and is connected to other universes, though sometimes the actions and reactions arising from it are less shocking than the surprises and frights that life sends our way.

Who doesn't know of someone who worked tirelessly all their life so they could retire, only to die shortly after retirement from an accident, a heart attack or cancer? Do we really have everything as firmly under control as we wish to believe deep down? At every waking moment, are we free to choose how we feel?

I fondly remember summer vacations when I was a kid. We would spend three months away from school and the city, in a small coastal village, just thirty feet from the seashore. I could run around more freely without being constantly monitored by my parents or teachers. I'd spend all day with my buddies, filled with adventure, discoveries and things we learned that made the time fly by.

There is one summer that I especially remember. We had started riding bikes, and I was thrilled about trying out a new yellow-and-red trials bike. I remember the time and place that a group of girls came up to me and how one of them sneered, "I know someone who's going to spend the whole summer alone on his new bike. Ha ha ha!"

Her words were like an arrow through my heart. It was just starting to heat up, and I imagined another epic summer on my new bike, far from home, racing through the fields, stealing melons and grapes with the gang. And suddenly, with that girl's words, I felt my expectations for the summer were squashed.

The pain of rejection and abandonment instilled by my family and teachers resurfaced. The resulting loneliness and feelings of guilt and shame had me in their grip. Once again, I had done something wrong and had to pay for it. As usual, I didn't know specifically what it was, but I didn't deserve to have what everyone else had.

I experienced the feeling of being excluded by authority figures and by my own group over and over until my early adolescence. It was a horrible feeling of being orphaned, being ostracized and, deep down, not belonging to anything respectable. I was constantly confused because I didn't know where I had gone *wrong* and felt incapable of getting things *right*. I was sure that I was a disgraceful outcast and a hopeless weirdo.

At fifteen, we were drinking alcohol and starting to use soft drugs. At night, with a warped sense of reality, I would pick fights all the time. It was something I couldn't stop doing, and I even enjoyed it, even though the others couldn't stand it and thought it was wrong. All this reinforced the belief that I had held for as long as I could remember: There was something wrong with me that I needed to change, but nobody ever told me exactly what that was. The boys of my summer gang warned me that if I kept acting the way I was, they wouldn't hang out with me anymore. But I couldn't understand why I was so provocative and reactive, and I was even more confused about how to change it.

According to mainstream psychology, we can change our feelings and actions right now by changing our thoughts. This is what our parents and teachers tried to do as children: change our way of being to fit the mold of what is proper, desirable and expected.

However, as our parents and teachers have surely experienced, many of our thoughts and our ways of being cannot be changed. Serginess is a product of the past, shaped by a personal history, and most of my thoughts are automatisms (automatic responses) that reflect my temperamental tendencies and unconscious learning.

Sergi Rufi was conditioned when he was three months old, nine months old, twenty-one years old and forty years old. It's true that I can change some of my thoughts. However, many of them come from scars and are part of my personality structure, just like my eye color and height are part of my physical structure.

Why do you get into trouble? Why do you talk so badly about yourself? Why do you fear what you like? Why do you hate what you're so attracted to? Why do you crave that food that makes you feel bad?

Our unconscious mind echoes our parents' voices in the present. The tone of the inner voice that speaks to us every day and the content of its messages are full of reproach, threats, fear and rigid rules and standards.

Our parents generally wanted the best for us, but they lacked any understanding of (**REAL**) psychology and child education, and the love they showed us was often erratic, disorganized, tense and chaotic.

They often punished us for our gifts and rewarded us for our outbursts. They belittled our achievements and applauded our irrational behavior. They didn't speak to us warmly, nor did they spend quality time with us or connect with us deeply. This is how our adult minds interact with us.

Originally, Serginess treated Sergi Rufi just like his father treated him (and Sergi Rufi treated Serginess the same way): in what felt like an authoritarian and contemptuous manner, which was how it treated others as well. We have inherited our chain of tension and negative interactions from our parents, and we carry its links into most of our relationships today.

Until we do deep inner work, taking a few steps back and traveling a bit inward, we replicate in the present the unfortunate legacy of the past. This can include bad luck, bad decisions, reprehensible actions and voices that sabotage us. Everything points back to the origin, to the first spin of the top.

In reality, the work has to be done with our own nervous system, and not with our actual parents. They don't have to change, or at least not directly, because we tell them to. It is we who must learn to relate to ourselves in a more adaptive way.

It is up to us to release the tension of chronic grief and trauma. We are not our parents' psychologists or counselors. Here and now, if I haven't done any inner work, I still carry my parents in my mind. Trace the tone of your childhood home through the tone of your thoughts.

In mainstream culture, urgency is the relational dynamic that colors interactions. Selling quick results and change is what feeds those at the top. Academic psychology cannot be separated from the environment in which it flourishes. Academic psychology is a product of the environment, and it advocates and takes a swift and superficial approach to human problems.

We must rationalize our emotions, change our thoughts and control our bodies. The top-down view has taken over, whereby what is above—our thoughts—controls what is below—our body. We are awash in Band-Aids and crutches. Though useful in certain situations, they are unlikely to help us grow and prosper, and more often than not, they are futile attempts at covering up a deeper wound.

In mainstream culture, the invisible world does not exist. The past must be left in the past (and this is actually true in some cases) because "it's a drag." Psychology bestsellers are written by journalists, engineers and spiritual gurus who mix up concepts and confuse people more than they help them. These people want to act like therapists to avoid seeing a therapist. But psychologists didn't study psychology to be happy or to know everything, so we must be wary of mental health professionals who only sell smiles, joy and order.

It is dark and cold in the depths of the Earth, of the oceans and the galaxy. As living beings, people experience joy, sadness, anger and fear. Most of these feelings are automatic and unconscious; they are a reflection of our nervous system, a wave of sensations that originate in our gut and rise to the mind in the form of thoughts. We can receive them, recognize them, understand them, release the discomfort they cause and change some parts of them. We must accept many others and learn to live in better harmony with who we are.

BECAUSE WE ARE THE RESULT OF MANY THINGS WE DIDN'T CHOOSE.

The idea that we must control our thoughts to be happy ends up controlling our lives. It becomes a deep hole, and with every effort we make to climb out, we end up digging ourselves a little deeper. This makes for a profitable business.

We think we are the **masters** of our bodies. We are under the illusion that we control our vision, our stomach and the circulation of our blood at will. But when something fails us and symptoms of illness appear, harsh reality rears its head. Then it is clear who is the master of whom, who controls whom, who leads and who follows.

We realize that we are not the masters of our liver when it fails us. The same goes for our personality: We cannot change it to suit our tastes. In a certain way, we don't have a personality so much as it has us. We have to understand it, forgive it and support it instead of struggling against it.

There are people with illnesses who try everything and die, people who don't take care of their health and live to be ninety. There are athletes with cancer and elderly people who smoke. Suicide can be found among the rich and longevity among the poor.

Everything is more mysterious, multicausal and complex than it seems. Only sensitivity, empathy and humility can bring us closer to the truth. There are things that we can change and others that we will have to learn to accept, sooner or later.

And it is especially important not to pontificate or

blame those who die, as if everything hinged on our effort, sacrifice, desire and willpower. The universe is vast, and we are governed and influenced by many different, variable forces. We need more humility and humanity, more support and less judgment. The end is already painful enough.

"If you're not happy with your girlfriend, leave her!" "If you don't like your job, quit!" "If you don't enjoy where you live, move!" So many recommendations are made based on the premise that **we can** change anything we want at any time (because we are free).

Knowing the best option, or even suspecting what might happen, is not the same as moving in that direction. Every nervous system has its own rhythm; it tunes in and out differently to the same circumstance. A lemon hanging from a branch knows it will end up on the ground or in the farmer's basket, but it doesn't know when. The same thing happens to us: We can guess at what we'll be thinking three minutes from now, but we don't know for sure.

Sometimes the prospect of loneliness hurts too much, and there are no other options. To tell someone, "If you don't love yourself, you don't love anyone," is to voice a cloaked sadistic opinion that, if expressed by a mental health professional, could cause *iatrogenic* harm.

If it were really so simple, people wouldn't need to see a psychologist. People don't come to us psychologists for "positive scolding," for paternalistic advice dripping with good intentions and rationalist simplifications. Such recommendations do not motivate people to take action. Instead, they often leave them feeling more stuck. When you force yourself to perform an action that was suggested to you, but that doesn't take into account your unique situation or the context of your upbringing, it's rarely sustainable in the long run. Eventually, a relapse occurs, and mainstream psychologists simply wash their hands of it.

Experts say that if we get lost in the woods, it's best to stay where we are. We shouldn't try to find our way out or we could get even more lost. The best thing to do is stay put and do nothing. Struggling, flailing around and running off into the wild makes it harder to be found within the first forty-eight hours.

So learning to wait and keeping calm (accepting the moment) rather than getting all worked up and overreacting (desperately trying to take control and change the situation) is often the best strategy both to survive and to thrive.

It seems that human beings are incomplete, like we're never quite finished. There's always something to work on, something that can be improved. You can always be thinner, stronger, healthier, younger and more beautiful. You can always sleep better, have a better sex life and be more spiritual.

Everything in mainstream culture is based on the idea that one can (and should) always improve. The values of constant self-improvement, at all costs, are the primary draw of YouTube channels, commercial self-help books and most spiritual workshops and retreats. But this pressure to **constantly improve** sets off an inner struggle against oneself.

There's always a gap to bridge between reality and your genetic potential, between what you are and what you could (and should) be. There is even a Spanish scientist who promotes the idea that aging is a disease.

In my practice, I've had hundreds of clients tell me the same story: "I showed my parents I got a B+ on a test, and they told me I had to get an A," and "I showed them I got an A on a test, and they told me it was the bare minimum." Can we appreciate our parents' stern tone and the tense kind of love they showed us to bring out the best in us? Is the absence of visible displays of affection clear? Can we detect the virus of constant self-improvement in us? Do we better understand now what our unconscious mind does to us? Our mind right now is only a replica and reflection of the past.

The prevailing mentality in society today is that of

the elite athlete. Athletes, entrepreneurs, models, actors, investors and millionaires with exceptional minds and bodies stand out in our digital world. They make a big splash and confuse those of us below them. "If I can do it, so can you." "If you want it, you can do it." "If you can't do it, it's because you don't want it badly enough."

They want to bring out the best in us, like our parents, using the same methods, the same stick and the same carrot: the pressure to constantly improve, based on effort and sacrifice, to win everyone's admiration by achieving astonishing results.

The sports athlete has become the father athlete, the wife athlete, the employee athlete, the entrepreneur athlete, the supervisor athlete, the student athlete and the gym athlete, staring in the mirror and holding back their emotions. Repressing people's humanity and promoting hard work for quick results destroys those at the bottom and further enriches those at the top.

"Pressure creates diamonds, and I'm going to shine," one athlete says with conviction at a press conference before the championship game. Of course, his rival is also a diamond, and anybody could get injured, suffer a heart attack, rupture an artery, get sick, end up with an addiction or have a panic attack.

Elite sports have been held up as an exemplary and ideal lifestyle for the rest of society. The values of high-performance sports are promoted to everyone. Some are fair enough, such as respect, health and determination. Others, such as extreme competitiveness, constant effort and sacrifice, are instilled in society as if they were harmless.

Coaches' gross abuse of athletes leads to parents' abuse of children and bosses' abuse of employees. Pushing and demanding better results leads to psychological injury.

"Go hard!" "Push it to the limit!" "Never give up!" The athlete's mindset applied to the field of psychology is dangerous. It creates androids, pawns, cogs in the machine, soldiers, hatchet men and everyday psychopaths. It produces hyperrationalized minds disconnected from their gut and their feelings.

They have learned to limit their vulnerability to their private life (and to deal with it alone). Or else they keep numbing it with substances and strenuous activity while pretending to be above the herd. No one suffers more than perfectionist, demanding and dissatisfied people. Those who stake their worth (their self-esteem) on a single competition once every two years turn their life into a game of chance.

This culture of pop perfectionism and self-imposed demand has spread from the Olympic Games and high-performance training centers to take root in families, schools, leisure time and social relationships. We want more, we believe we can achieve more and we demand more of ourselves.

We have more results, more trophies and more medals, while companies, bosses and the government rub their hands and profit at our expense.

EVERYONE WANTS MORE PRODUCTION AND MORE RESULTS AT THE EXPENSE OF THE MENTAL HEALTH OF THOSE AT THE BOTTOM.

"I don't have the time." "I've wasted time." "I'm running out of time." "I'm late." The illusion of wasting time is a consequence of the pressure for constant self-improvement. If I've stayed the same, if I've held steady, it means I haven't made the most of my time.

If I take a nap, I'm wasting time. If I lie on the couch, I'm wasting time. If I'm not producing tangible results, I'm wasting time. If I'm not learning something new, I'm wasting time. How often were we told as children that our hobbies and interests were a waste of time?

When I was a boy, we spent eighty percent of the school day in the classroom. A small amount of time and space were set aside for rest and leisure. The authorities who designed the draconian curricula are the same as those who tell us to "relax" and "just deal with it" when things don't work out for us as adults.

Doctors, nurses, lawyers, janitors and taxi drivers all mouth this advice while keeping their real thoughts to themselves.

If we go for a walk, we're wasting our time. If we type on a computer, we're investing in our future. Does anyone know how to calmly not do anything in particular?

After working with many clients, I have come to realize that it's highly likely that when we think we're investing our time well by doing what others expect of us, we're actually wasting it. And when we think we're wasting our time by doing things that fulfill us and bring us joy, we're investing it better.

Becoming the best version of yourself is the slogan that excites and disturbs us the most. Who came up with the widespread expectation that we must be better at something (if not everything) with each passing day? Plants and animals go through the entire cycle of life in silence.

However, mainstream culture (science, politics, religion, social media, the self-help industry and commercial media) puts so much pressure on us to become the best version of ourselves. To pursue this ideal, we end up believing it is an essential part of life that our birth is followed by a fixed state of grace, fulfillment, constant learning and abundance.

And if that isn't the case, it's because there's something wrong with us. And so we go along with the world, subjecting ourselves to demands for constant self-improvement that end up frustrating us all the time while we pretend to be immortal, happy and special.

In reality, our "best version" will often emerge regardless of our own wishes and the efforts of cultural programming. It will come about spontaneously, and sometimes when we are on our deathbed, just moments before taking our last breath. "I'm sorry. I couldn't have done it any better. I love you." May such a display of humanity and sensitivity appear in our lives long before our swan song.

Ultimately, there is no better version of ourselves than the one most appropriate to each situation. At a funeral, we connect with sadness. At a comedy show, we experience joy. When we meet with friends, we express ourselves openly and share. During a job interview, we measure our words and adapt what we say to that specific context. When it's time to work, we work, and when it's time to rest, we rest.

Homeostasis as such does not exist; we would be better off talking about *homeokinesis*, a fragile balance that is constantly moving and readjusting in a flexible, ever-changing flow. This internal back and forth is typical of people who allow themselves to connect and live according to the lower pathway (the train tracks), which is connected to our values (the overhead power cable).

Our feelings and principles guide us along the way. We are receptive to contact, to learning, to reaffirming and evolving. We are open to experience.

Personally, I'm not trying to be the best version of myself. I would rather feel more comfortable being myself in any situation.

If you turn on the television, almost everyone speaks, looks, smiles, dresses, jokes, "reasons" and shouts in the same way. If you go to the mall, many people move, express themselves and resemble the people you see on television. Something similar happens wherever big crowds of people gather: You clearly see uniformity, **conformity** and a lack of individuality, authenticity and independent thought.

Most people like the same song (the one played twenty times a day on the radio), want the same thing (whatever today's most popular influencer is promoting) and seek the same thing in a partner (whatever today's most popular dating coach is calling for). Mainstream culture designs a single mold and convinces us that by **fitting** it, we will feel better understood and more protected by the community. However, we just end up becoming more predictable and malleable, and ultimately more confused.

Mainstream culture has created a changing, insecure and liquid world where anxiety flows into every aspect of life: money, work, love and the future. What lies beyond social media culture and the forced smile? Adapting to this normalcy leads us to settle for dystopian work environments, group bullying, burnout and superhuman syndrome. The exemplary heroine is perfect at everything. She is a good worker, decisive, uncritical, productive, a good friend, daughter, mother and the ideal partner.

Even though no biological **mold** is better than any other, mainstream culture clearly shows a preference for one way of being over others. The personality that best adapts to mainstream customs is preferred. It is the most successful and the most widespread. It is also the most manageable and easiest to influence. The *evolutive* mind clashes with life, while the *replicative* mind flows better.

If you are sensitive, thoughtful and profound, but are told that something about you doesn't fit the mold, then trying to change or restructure your ideas in a way that more closely aligns with mainstream culture results in self-monitoring and overthinking. The same thing happens with rumination, nervousness and tension. Focusing on our thoughts increases the flow of thoughts, which ends up overwhelming us.

This also occurs with journaling or putting thoughts down on paper. These are "therapeutic" tools based on a top-down (upper pathway) view of the human experience. Underlying them is the assumption that we can control our feelings by controlling what we think. Most superfluous obsessions and worries are produced by these types of strategies.

We are not all the same. Superficial people who lack insight into themselves and are emotionally deprived might initially find these techniques useful for understanding themselves better. But if they continue to delve deeper, they will end up increasing the flow of thoughts, which will lead to greater frustration and *iatrogenic* harm from *replicative* mental health professionals.

Similarly, techniques such as visualization, meditation or even yoga can help us recognize, feel and pay more attention to our bodies. This can be beneficial for people when starting on their inner journey. However, excessive **self-observation** can lead us to feel and experience too much of ourselves, with a sense that we are trapped in our own bodies. This can trigger hypochondriacal, phobic and even psychotic tendencies.

Every solution has a biphasic effect: What relieves us in small doses punishes us when we take larger doses.

Focusing on something helps us a little, just as *defocusing* does at the right time. Attention and distraction, like memory and forgetting, are manifestations of the same thing.

If you are *evolutive*, sensitive and thoughtful, you will surely find something that fits your personality and tendencies to be more useful. The practical tools (or lack thereof) will be those that best fit your particular mold. Prescribed methods are of no use to you; the cultural mold excludes much of your rich identity because it fails to understand it. Therefore, it limits and blames you. Each individual benefits from a different type of practice or technique.

After thirteen years of daily spiritual practice (and three years during which I gave it up), I can say that meditation is best suited to taciturn and phlegmatic people. These are people who are habitually quiet, reserved and silent. They are emotionally subdued, closed off, introverted and even cold. Nothing is right for everyone, nothing is harmless and the success of any method is closely related to its dosage.

It's also normal if meditation makes you more nervous or if yoga bores you. You can walk in nature, do stretching at home, play relaxing music, swim with your dog or engage in forest bathing,[1] and if that's what checks your boxes, then you'll arrive at the same place. The goal is to feel your nervous system become greener, calmer and more balanced.

And by doing so, you'll understand yourself better, because silence allows us to connect with the depths of our being, with our instinct for creativity and compassion. It doesn't matter whether it's an ancient practice or something more of your own making. What focuses, awakens or enlightens one person can disorient, bore or confuse another. We can always suggest, indicate or inspire, but we can't impose strict guidelines on anyone.

The concept of well-being that's sold to us is also problematic. Well-being is associated with being productive. "Today I feel good. I had a productive day," we say when we feel good.

However, actions that don't relate to productivity like reading a book we enjoy, eating well, taking a nap or walking along an empty beach can fill us with pleasant sensations, and they don't convey a sense of being commodified.

When I feel good or when I am enjoying what I

---

1 Forest bathing (*shinrin-yoku*) is a Japanese therapeutic practice that involves slowly and mindfully walking in a forest environment while fully engaging all five senses.

am doing, I feel free (a sensation). Our well-being is the momentary result of many things coming together that we cannot perceive, control or explain.

And without realizing it, we end up attributing everything to productivity. If I haven't produced anything, I feel bad, and even guilty, because people who don't do anything don't produce, and people who don't produce don't deserve to feel good.

Ultimately, trying to make every day good is what makes the hard days feel truly miserable. In the end,

"KNOWING HOW TO LOSE" IS A GIFT THAT HELPS US TO "WIN" IN THE LONG RUN.

When spirituality makes you feel guilty for not meeting expectations, when it forces you to strive for greater perfection, when it makes you repress yourself more, it has become a disorganized religion. If there is no love involved, it isn't spirituality.

It's highly reputable to position yourself online as spiritual. It gives you a new purpose, it looks good, it gets you likes, it gives you power and it makes you feel superior. It feels good when people think of your spirituality and closeness to the truth as charming and admirable.

However, trying to dissolve your ego, then bragging about having done so is the first symptom of the spiritual narcissist and the false guru.

Guru syndrome compensates for imposter syndrome. These two extremes complement each other. The more insecure one feels inside, the more outlandish and exaggerated their spiritual posturing will be to present themselves as flawless.

Until the twentieth century, enlightenment was a silent, private and transformative inner experience. Now, in the twenty-first century, it's a profitable exhibitionist business suitable for all consumers.

Controlling our thoughts is mainstream psychology's marketing mirage. Transcending emotions is an illusion promoted by **commercial spirituality**. Nobody can dissolve their nervous system.

No spiritual practice that isolates, separates or distances us is therapeutic. Spiritual practice heals when it helps us reconcile, unite and enhance our social sensitivity and awareness—when it makes us more polite and respectful of public space and the environment. It's what brings us down from the mountain and makes us connect more with others.

Our inner voice is the internalization of the often demanding voices of authority we heard as children. They wanted us to obey their rules or they would make us feel guilty.

If you're polite and sensitive, you probably have (or have had) a voice that monitors your behavior, pointing out your mistakes and prodding you to do better. At first, it reminded us to do our homework and scolded us for being lazy. Later, it warned us to be more productive or we'd get fired.

These days, it pressures us to meditate, do yoga, eat better, drink better, sleep better, smile more, think positively, behave well, be politically correct, be grateful, show enthusiasm and act as if nothing is standing in our way.

Under social influence, we have developed a critical and demanding inner voice that follows us everywhere, insisting on a level of perfection that is impossible to achieve. Our inner parent later became our inner boss and is now our **inner guru**.

On top of our financial, work-related and emotional obligations, we now have a spiritual duty as well. We must accomplish everything now more than ever. Spiritual obsessions have spread with the emergence of social media culture.

This exacting expectation, imposed by mainstream culture and absorbed by the *replicative* mind, builds a society with more anxiety, shame and guilt for being unable to reach what is upheld as the perfect moral ideal.

We have to fail that guru. We must disappoint him,

just as we may have disappointed our parents. Let's not try to take on any more consciousness, intelligence or sensitivity than our organism can sustain and manage. We have exactly the right amount of what we can deal with right now.

It's only a matter of time before we evolve. Sometimes, it will coincide with an act of will. Other times, life will force it upon us. But we can't speed it up deliberately, or we'll pay dearly.

Ten years ago, a shaman told me I wasn't ready for astral travel, and I ignored her. My curiosity and recklessness always won out over my patience and caution. The huge mess I got myself into only confirmed that my body is more fragile than my attitude and that it can't sustain it.

Both a lack of training and an excess of experience can overwhelm us.

Understanding

Peace cannot be kept by force; it can only be achieved by understanding.

Albert Einstein

My long years as a psychotherapist have made me realize that many people (more than we might imagine) still bear the consequences of **traumatic** experiences from childhood.

Many of our parents were **traumatized** by their own parents. We have parents with mental disorders, parents with addictions, parents with poor emotional management skills, financially challenged parents, absent parents, parents living in poverty, codependent parents and emotionally overwhelmed parents. Many of us are children of divorce. Many of us grew up with domestic violence, and our parents may have died or lived with chronic grief. Many of us were abused psychologically, physically and/or sexually by authority figures, which has hindered our psychological development.

Whether acute or chronic, these episodes have left their emotional imprint on us and shaped our nervous system's response to our environment, directly influencing what we like and dislike, how we relate to ourselves, how we take care of ourselves, how we neglect ourselves, and how we talk with and meet people, make friends, and form romantic relationships. Furthermore, many **traumas** are invisible, unspoken, denied, repudiated or projected onto others.

You can consider yourself fortunate if, as the poet Rainer Maria Rilke said, childhood is your homeland, because for many, it was hell. It was the place where many received the least affection, understanding, respect, security and protection. Many were not taught knowledge, values, manners, ethics, character development, emotional management skills, critical thinking or the ability to generate and maintain their own income. They were not given the tools necessary to develop into adults capable of thriving emotionally and financially.

Furthermore, eighty percent of sexual abuse takes place within the family. We were squeezed through an insensitive and authoritarian educational system where bullying was normalized. Then we entered an unstable job market where we endure economic exploitation, workplace bullying and burnout.

Mainstream culture has created a social system weak in deep communication and warm and healthy relationships. As a result of this emptiness, lack of understanding and connection, many of us have felt alone, helpless, uprooted, orphaned and emotionally homeless. This feeling of alienation has been quietly passed down from generation to generation. We haven't felt loved or important.

We tripped and fell and nobody picked us up from the ground, our hugs were forced, and our mother's caresses were few and far between. Those ashamed, self-conscious and guilt-ridden children have grown into disoriented, lost and unhinged adults.

Two people get into a traffic dispute that ends in a knife fight. A teenager jumps off a bridge after being ridiculed by his classmates for the umpteenth time. A motorcyclist snatches an elderly woman's purse, and she breaks her neck as she falls backward. A girl is gang-raped by a group of boys. A man blasts music every night and won't let his neighbors rest. Most of these extreme behaviors involve extreme trauma.

We can't help but get addicted to video games, our phones, television, sugar, toxic love and pornography. In a culture where nothing is guaranteed, where everything is designed to overstimulate us and push us off center, it's natural for our nervous system to be hyperactivated, constantly tense and on guard. Considering the minds we've inherited and the betrayals and bitterness we've endured, we're doing quite well.

There are situations or contexts that cause stress, psychological tension and anxiety in most people.

These are **universal stressors**: finals week, oral exams, the driving test, speaking in public, grieving the end of a relationship, nursing a broken heart, having problems at work, losing your job, being unemployed, moving to a new city, moving to a new country, adapting to a new culture, sitting in traffic, wedding preparations, the wedding day, getting bullied, getting ganged up on, getting harassed by a parent, teacher or boss, planning a vacation, the death of a loved one, the early stages of a romantic relationship, and unrequited love (or sexual desire).

These are scenarios that most of us have experienced or will experience. They tip us off balance emotionally because their demands exceed our ability to manage them, and they hyperactivate our nervous system's fight-or-flight response. At these times, we may feel threatened, incapable, vulnerable, restless or grumpy. And we may overthink or fixate on the situation, shut down or feel like we're at a loss.

It is crucial to recognize these situations as "normal" (because they happen frequently, not because they are desirable) and avoid adding fuel to the fire when they come up. At these times, you have to keep your inner critic in check. It is unfair to use these extreme moments to criticize, devalue and blame yourself, just as your parents, teachers and bosses used to do to you.

Let's not heap more shame and guilt onto situations that almost everyone experiences, that affect and upset us all, and that are not directly related to any personal failure or trauma. Life is already tough enough.

The allure of the **search** is too tempting. It is an enticing prospect for something greater that promises to heal childhood traumas, end universal stressors and help you manage the tedium of everyday life. On the other bank of the river of mediocrity is a golden place where it is always warm and full of satisfying relationships.

Searching allows us to distract ourselves and temporarily escape from the present moment. It connects us with feelings of hope, relief, adventure and freedom. It offers a sense of newness, improvement, movement, control and the ability to manage our choices.

When I was a teenager, I stumbled across a CD in a music store called *The Mind Is a Terrible Thing to Taste* by the group Ministry. I didn't understand what that meant at the time, but the words left me spellbound. I wasn't yet aware of my personal problems, and I didn't know anything about psychology. Still, the line stuck with me.

I later heard that the front man was addicted to heroin and understood what the album's title meant. Decades later, I realized that you didn't even have to be addicted to drugs; if you push things too far, your mind can become a living hell. After all, we live inside our minds. We are made of our mind. We are our mind, and our mind is us.

At some point along our inner journey, searching further than necessary into the mind becomes counterproductive. The psychological benefit is minimal, and the risk of obsession is high. Mount Everest's twenty-nine thousand feet are child's play compared to the yawning distance separating us from the summit within.

Studying the mind feels like trying to solve a puzzle. When you ignore your thoughts, they appear. When you attempt to rationalize them, they vanish. It is a delocalized phenomenon, not confined to any specific place. It exists in many places and none, all at the same time. It is a mirror, a sponge. It is a dark and sealed empty box. It is a universe of its own, full of black holes and supernovae.

Unless you are a psychologist or a shaman, it's better to spare yourself the stress that comes with **searching** for the ultimate, metaphysical **truth**, trying to understand the deep meaning of life or exploring the outer limits of the mind. Most Westerners in the twenty-first century are missionaries more than mystics. Our nervous system works best in the physical world of everyday life and worse when it is absorbed in an intangible and hypothetical one.

We can theorize about the mind and the afterlife, but we cannot experience both deeply and return intact. If you penetrate the labyrinth of the mind, you should know that it is as slippery as mercury and as sharp as a razor. Sooner or later, you will end up facing the madness, in search of concepts or ideas that are meaningless in the real world.

LOOKING INWARD CAN FEEL COMFORTING AT FIRST, BUT IT CAN BECOME TORTUROUS IN THE LONG RUN.

If you close up and withdraw too deeply into yourself, you'll end up self-centered, self-observant, hypervigilant and obsessed with your sensations and feelings. You'll be more tense, more self-referential, more activated and more trapped within the walls of your body. You'll be more anxious. And if you're not, just read about the lives of the Christian mystics Saint John of the Cross or Saint Teresa of Ávila, and you'll see how much they struggled.

It's only a matter of time before we stumble upon traces of childhood traumas and markers of everyday stressors. We all carry them to a greater or lesser extent.

Life is already complicated enough. The job market is tight, pay is low and prices are high. Relationships are fickle, bonds don't last and loneliness is everywhere. The present is unstable, and the future is uncertain. Existential crises are all the rage, but psychiatric disorders terrify us, and both intertwine, overlap and share symptoms.

We have only one brain and one nervous system for

our entire lifetime. By pushing them to the limit, overstressing them, frightening and wearing them down, we risk spending the rest of our days limping along, broken and paying a steep price. We can go from balance to imbalance, from exposure to flooding and retraumatization, in the blink of an eye.

After thirteen years of daily spiritual practice, using different proven techniques for contemplation and expanding consciousness, you come back to square one. The myth of the Hero's Journey ends with the same nervous system in tatters. We search for ways to alleviate our illnesses and disorders, and each of us end up with our own. Boundaries only appear after we have crossed them, and by then, it's too late.

The tangible and applicable truth is what makes our nervous system feel calm, balanced and secure with itself, with people and with the world around it.

At the end of our sessions, I always recommend that my clients go outside for at least ten minutes, take a walk and get some fresh air. It's crucial for them to leave behind the abstractions of their mind, with their eyes closed, visualizing and contemplating, and return to movement, with their eyes open, stimulated by the specific details of everyday life.

This is when I make significant progress, once I've stepped outside myself and put my feet back on the ground.

What is more important than where we're going is how long we plan to stay there. Our peak spiritual or mystical experiences depend on their intensity and length. At some point, prolonged exposure turns into torture.

There is no panacea out there, and nothing about playing with the mind and the nervous system is harmless. This is even more the case when it comes to spiritual practice and the search for the supposed ultimate truth.

We are born with a **body** (zygote, fetus, embryo, infant), and we die with a body (corpse). In between, we develop thought, language, understanding, communication, consciousness and individual identity to a greater or lesser extent.

Therefore, before we are conscious beings, we are unconscious beings. Before we are rational beings, we are emotional beings. Before we are autonomous beings, we are social beings. First comes our body, then comes our mind. First comes sensation, then comes thought. First comes our physiological response, then comes our psychological understanding. Without the mind, there is still a body (deep sleep and comatose states). Without the body, there is no mind (from a practical point of view, at least).

Similarly, if we go back further, all the way to the beginning of the existence of life on Earth, we were reptiles before we were mammals, we were mammals before we were primates, and we were primates before we were humans. The deep brain (reptilian and primate: instinct and emotion) has a stronger pull on our impulses, responses and behaviors than our human brain (thoughts and will).

Our brain is the consequence of billions of years of biological transformation. Our current tastes, responses and behaviors are the summary of countless interactions between what we have inherited and the contexts that have influenced us. We are the result of the norms and conditioning we have received from our family, schooling, culture and society.

Therefore, we feel first and think second. Some people are unaware of this automatic process, or they use thought as a way to feel their body, while others feel so much that they can't put it into words. We are complex beings. Some lean toward rational control of unconscious processes (the illusion of control), while others are more in touch with the lower pathway, feeling and sensation.

We generally have trouble accepting the unconscious and emotional parts of ourselves because we fear them. We don't understand it. We want to erase the traumas of our past and cover up our wounds, denying them with rituals and words of affirmation. However, our feelings pay no heed to such intentions. We can't rid ourselves of the factors that make us the way we are, just because we want to.

We feel insecure when we are vulnerable, uncomfortable with the idea of being fallible. We perceive our extreme fragility as weakness.

How could I like someone like *that*? Why do I feel anything when I don't even know her? Why do I think about her so much if we're still nothing? We feel bad about the lower pathway, about feeling, sensitivity and the sense that we are **mammals**, longing for connection and emotionally dependent on others.

These are the needs of our **inner mammal**, which throbs, stirs, yearns and lives in us, within and below, without us ever realizing that it's the one calling the shots. This inner mammal longs for emotional bonding, meaningful skin-to-skin contact, attunement, listening, attention, connection with others, communion, praise, the group, the pack and a home.

Why do you feel jealousy? Because the bond with this person is important to you, and you're afraid their bond with someone else might be stronger, just like what happened to you in the past. You did not choose this feeling; it's triggered in your body, and your mind simply recognizes it. By acknowledging it, you end up blaming yourself for experiencing that natural and automatic emotion. This is how we were raised. This is how mainstream culture has placed blame on our nervous system.

Personally, however, the times I've felt jealous, I've never done anything about it. And I definitely don't do what my frightened thoughts urge me to do. I just observe my fear and acknowledge it. I don't deceive myself or try to restructure what I think. The thought thinks (itself) inside me, but I don't think it deliberately. I don't choose it, and it doesn't even have much to do with me in the present moment.

And I try not to react the way my frightened and ashamed mind goads me to. I don't try to control my mind or my body, just as I don't try to control the wind even though I'd prefer it blew in a different direction. I don't try to control anything or anyone. I allow myself to be, I allow others to be and I let things happen. I observe, and I understand how the ancient and complex ascending mechanism of the human experience works.

And if I can, I communicate, I express myself and I share the movement of my nervous system with the nervous system of the other person. We work well; Serginess wants to protect me to prevent something bad from happening to me again. I suffered so much then. And I whisper gratitude to it and remind it that it's in the past. We're safe now, and what happened then won't happen again.

"I realize I need approval, and I don't like that." "It bothers me when things affect me." "Things shouldn't affect me so much. I get so frustrated with myself." "I have to be strong." Many clients have shared such feelings with me over the decades.

Mainstream psychology (cognitive restructuring and the illusion of mental control) and New Age, Disneyfied doctrine (overly positive thinking, plastic smiles and esoteric practices) create people who struggle against the fragility of their nervous system. In doing so, they seem to reject their own humanity by denying the neurophysiological basis of their thinking, emotions and behavior.

They are in conflict with their inner mammal, viewing its expression as a sign of weakness and inadequacy. They are ashamed of their emotions and of feeling vulnerable. They think there's something wrong with them that they need to fix. They chase the illusion of becoming insensitive androids or grandiloquent gods who have risen above their primate origins and attained the static and aesthetic well-being of social media.

Just as my dog, Víctor, needs my support to move around in open spaces and make decisions that don't put him in danger, we also need company when we feel vulnerable.

We need the warmth of people who understand us, the support of those who love us for who we are, without trying to change us or criticize us for our weirdness. Seeking the approval of our inner circle is a sign of accepting who we are (mammals who need their pack) and a reflection of mental health.

The opposite of this is the madness of false self-sufficiency (being completely independent beings, with no need for relationships with other humans), which deep down leads to a greater sense of loneliness. And to escape this loneliness, we need to erect our walls even higher, turn up the volume on our headphones, avoid eye contact, grimace, stare more at the screen, puff out our chests and clench our jaws to appear more confident and determined. It's the vicious cycle of self-isolation: The more I isolate myself, the more self-conscious and embarrassed I feel in public, and the more I need to isolate myself. That's living **against** our mammalian instincts.

It is important to discover what we like and what we don't, what turns us on and what turns us off energetically.

What **instrument** would you be in an orchestra? What appliance would you be at home? In what kinds of conditions, in which types of situations and with which kinds of people do you function best?

What types of foods and mealtimes are best for you? What season, climate and temperature make you feel most active and alive? At what time of day do you feel most clear-headed or most confused? How many hours of sleep do you need?

What level of stress can you endure without breaking down? What type of exercise suits you and how often? What type of work is the best use of your talents? What level of noise pollution can you tolerate? What lifestyle is most appropriate for your nervous system? How much money do you need to live a life that works for you?

In an orchestra, I'd be the double bass. You don't always hear it, but you can feel it, even if few are aware of it. If the double bass is silent, the whole orchestra sounds empty. In a band, I'd be a singer with synthesizers. Pure passion and words. Tell me your musical style and I'll tell you who you are; give me your favorite playlist and I'll tell you what you're like. Was your favorite playlist discovered by your nervous system (the lower pathway), or was it chosen for you by mainstream radio and television (pounding it over and over again until you felt like it was your own)?

I've been a rock lover since I was fourteen, and I was a punk rocker until I was twenty-five. Then my nervous system opened up to other genres and began to feel swayed by electronic music, intimate pop, electropop, classical music, ambient music and so on. From a very early age, Latin rhythms seemed to mount an assault on my physiology. Serginess also has problems with the cadence of classic jazz. Quick, light, excessively cheerful, disordered and unpredictable music throws my nervous system off balance. Serginess prefers subtle emotion, elaborate lyrics, a deep message and a simple yet elaborate groove that gently pushes forward.

My favorite music is the kind that lifts me from the bottom up. It reveals the lower pathway (Serginess). It gives me goose bumps and feels effortless. It gives me a burst of clarity, lifting and inspiring me. I get the desire to create, write, travel and move. In that moment, I am the music, and I feel life fade into the background. I feel a sense of relief. Finished, impossibly intricate paragraphs, fresh perspectives on old situations and new conclusions arise in my mind.

When music resonates with my nervous system, sound and dance become one. It triggers a flood of memories, and the separate streams of my life flow together. I am bathed in the calm green light, and order and meaning emerge from the depths, like the periscope of a submarine.

When Sergi Rufi tries to push Serginess (condescendingly), the possibility of a new trauma opens up. However, when the movement of the sound goes upward, starting from the bottom up, life fits together, and what needs to happen, happens. The reality of your nature is never wrong. Thoughts and desires often are.

It is important that we explore and experiment to discover our own unique instrument and learn how to play it, tune it and refine our sound. Embrace curiosity along with your fear, but remain respectful of the structure or it could break. We each have a talent, and two or three at most. We also have a purpose, an overarching goal or direction. Exploring and discovering it with humility helps us to avoid problems and makes our lives easier. The direction and tempo are indicated by our nervous system.

Inside, I'm not free. I don't decide my feelings, my sensations, my thoughts, my body temperature, my digestion speed, when I need to go to the bathroom or when I'm hungry. Inside, I must learn to **allow** neurochemical processes to occur and to trust my mind–body organism.

Everything within me has a protective function, including pain, cramps, hiccups, sneezing, fatigue, sadness and my thoughts. Everything is managed deep within me and surfaces outward. I'm learning to **let everything happen within me**. I listen to my thoughts, I observe my emotional state and I manage it if necessary. If I do it the other way around and rationalize the feeling before I actually have it, I stifle it and build more tension.

My body and my mind should be like an open window where everything appears and disappears, everything comes in and out, pushed by the wind that life blows through my nervous system.

I embrace everything that emerges, happens and unfolds within. Viewing my internal processes as a cellular byproduct of being alive allows me to experience Serginess without guilt, as I don't have to repress anything. Essentially, everything begins in our inner cavity; what we can see is merely a reflection, an image or a reaction from within. It can also be a lie if I try to change it or fake it to appear otherwise.

At this point, I understand what works for me and what doesn't, what feels good for my body and what doesn't. If onions don't sit well with me, it only makes sense that I don't eat them. If wool doesn't feel good on my skin, I don't buy it. I allow myself to be who I am; I stop forcing what I can't change, and I don't evade the inevitable.

I lean into the breeze of life, which helps me and blows in my favor. To do this, I better understand Serginess; I stop struggling against it, even if it doesn't fit the mold of mainstream expectations. I take care of myself. Life is hard, which is why I make it easier for myself.

WHAT I ALLOW MYSELF, I MAKE NATURAL; WHAT I FORBID MYSELF, I ASSOCIATE WITH GUILT.

We can transform how we feel, but not what we are. We can change certain habits and behaviors, but our nervous system only affords us a tight margin. As the product of our genes and upbringing, we can understand ourselves and regulate ourselves better. We understand that we all need to experience connection and belonging to feel balanced. Quantity and quality are personal and non-transferable. It makes no sense to follow protocols to the letter or to adhere to closed methods, because the causes came before and are multifactorial. We are not the cause of anything, but merely a link or a continuation. Therefore, we are blameless. We are a response—another consequence and automatic reaction that we have learned to recognize, decipher and manage better.

To let things happen within is to treat the inevitable as natural and to forgive ourselves. It is to recognize that inside we were never free. It is to burst the dam of repression, releasing the stagnant waters of the past through the flow of the present.

Our experiences provide a degree of self-knowledge that informs our standards. We need to continue experimenting, negotiating between the seams of our own criteria and what life brings. With flexibility, negotiation and adaptation, we can get there, bit by bit.

It is crucial to understand the mismatch between our natural internal functioning and the drumbeat of mainstream culture. If we are aware of the disconnect between biology and culture, and if we summon enough courage, we will often have to swim against the cultural tide to stay true to our own nature. This is what we must do to protect our mental health and maintain our integrity.

We've been made to feel guilty about leisure. When we stop producing or are less efficient, just so we can rest or enjoy something passively, we become less worthy. For a day to be productive, we must have achieved, accomplished or learned something.

I understand that most people don't analyze their physical environment or their inner world. Some may examine their surroundings, but few really peer within. Observation is frowned upon. Though I had explained in earlier chapters that looking *too* deeply within yourself can cause more harm than good, mainstream culture prefers that we avoid introspection at all, as it already assigns us its opinions, standards and tastes. It persuades us to believe that it's better for us to focus on following its rules and being *replicative*.

However, those who are born (or learn to be) sensitive, thoughtful and/or introspective are more acutely aware that they reside within their own inner world and recognize the signals of their nervous system. They know that their way of feeling and desiring springs from an automatic source. Control is a partial, fleeting, erratic and frustrating feeling.

The insensitive believe in television and the headlines. Sometimes they're right, but they often repeat mistakes and validate utopian clichés spread far and wide by mainstream psychology ("think positive and you'll live well") and insincere, unrealistic platitudes ("the whole universe is on your side"). Those with rich inner lives have their own thoughts and are conscious; those who rely on external signaling conform to and parrot mainstream groupthink.

I understand that we live much of our lives spontaneously. It's also clear that we cannot force spontaneity or make it happen by an act of will—we have to foster and support it instead. Plants grow from the inside out and from the bottom up. For *evolutive* people, curiosity, experimentation, exploration, connection and play are standard. We are our own guinea pigs, testing grounds, databases and laboratories.

I understand that traveling, reading, investigating, reflecting, listening, questioning and connecting with human diversity make it easier to understand everyone's circumstances better: those who commit crimes, people who are deemed outcasts, those without homes or wealth. We can understand their background and their conditions, their origins and their perspectives, their potential and the reasons behind their actions. We can put ourselves in most people's shoes; few issues are totally foreign to us. We can acknowledge that we would surely react similarly given the same resources.

I understand that when someone commits a crime, they must pay for it, either with a fine or through spending time incarcerated. However, blaming them for their own circumstances is also misunderstanding their humanity. Without education and knowledge, with a poor upbringing and no employment prospects, I might have fallen into the same trap. Nobody plans to commit a crime and end up in the grave before their time.

Every addiction tells a story, and every drama can be traced back to its traumas. Did a criminal choose to be born into a family of criminals? Is a crack addict guilty for never knowing his father? Is a homeless person guilty of being born to a mother hooked on heroin? There's always a story underneath that the casual observer cannot see. *Replicative* people are unaware of this and only judge based on the present, ignorant of past causes. What would they do if they traded places?

I've met brilliant people at Harvard and brilliant people working in construction, brilliant people in church and brilliant people sweeping streets, brilliant people addicted to sports and brilliant people addicted to drugs, brilliant people in Malibu and brilliant people in a Roma village. Intelligence, like personality, character, willpower and effort, does not arise disconnected from certain conditions, contexts or traditions or a specific mainstream culture.

After **real understanding** comes **compassion**. Guilt culture gets it all backwards. Few feel compassion for themselves. Compassion is followed by humility, gratitude, forgiveness and acceptance of what we cannot choose and cannot change, no matter how much we may want to.

However, too much understanding poses its own dilemma. Bit by bit, it overwhelms us, entangling us in a web of paralyzing doubt, bogging us down in the illusory swamp of unlimited possibility and in obsessive *information toxicity*.

Until the twentieth century, the common concept of **maturity and adulthood**, based on a *replicative* morality, meant having a job, starting a family, making money, knowing how to save, blending in, being very responsible, having children, advocating values (both leading by example and not leading by example), maintaining your composure in public, keeping your emotions private, knowing how to solve problems independently, getting along with your family, following your family's rules and traditions, not causing conflicts or problems, having good manners, adhering to convention, maintaining your social image, making a good impression, ensuring that people speak well of you, not causing concern, not letting on that anything bothers you in public, fitting in well with the community, replicating customs, meeting your family's expectations, not showing vulnerability in public and showing love only with words or actions.

But a new concept of maturity emerged in the twenty-first century, based on an *evolutive* morality. It meant having your own opinion, questioning authority, not believing everything reported in the mainstream media, managing your emotions, sharing your feelings, having your own values, being consistent (advocating values and leading by example), doing inner work, making money, becoming morally independent from your family, showing sensitivity when appropriate, asking for help and favors when necessary, helping others when asked, being true to yourself, contradicting others when necessary, asking for forgiveness when appropriate, trying not to blame or accept being blamed, breaking with convention when appropriate, being able to say what you think, saying "I love you" and meaning it, showing love with words and actions and disappointing your family when the situation calls for it.

Maturity, in this sense, is linked to feeling deeply and prioritizing privacy, freedom and autonomy.

Truth and change are complex processes, like sleeping and love. They cannot be brought about by an act of will or forced by rational thought. They are organic, sensitive and subtle phenomena, like the changing tide or the arrival of spring. They simply happen, little by little or all at once. Sometimes you have to stop doing so much and learn to wait—learn to find the right place and time.

Change is possible, but also limited. You can change your job, your relationships, where you live and your habits. Internally, this involves a shift in perspective and understanding, including greater knowledge, better emotional management and more effective communication. It's not that difficult. The seed lies within us and just needs to be discovered, fertilized and watered.

By late adolescence or early adulthood, the ship is already built. Some ships are equipped to venture into intercontinental waters, while others anchor off the coast or in reservoirs. Understanding our capabilities and limitations, and dispelling self-delusion, is our main goal.

We can change the sheet metal and the paint, but we have little leeway to change the structure, the control panel and the boiler. We must respect the ship's capacity, its endurance and the nature of the journey chosen for us to undertake.

We can't change the world, despite what politicians say. We can't change the past, as promised by this New Age, romanticized doctrine. We can't change human beings. We can't change our parents, our temperament or our personality.

WE MUST ALLOW THE INEVITABLE, STOP TRYING TO FORCE THE IMPOSSIBLE AND LEARN TO BE AT PEACE WITH WHO WE ARE.

Values

Guilt is about as useful as a
dog's bite on a stone.

Commonly attributed to Sigmund Freud

No child has ever been born guilty. However, few elderly people die without guilt or remorse.

When we were children, we were singled out for our physical appearance, for our haircut or acne. We were criticized for how we spoke, thought, dressed, saw things, walked, felt, expressed emotions and related to others.

We were made to feel ashamed about our bodies, our thoughts, our sexuality, our actions and our reactions. We were told we were too sensitive, too shy or too cold.

We grew up hearing others complain about us. "You're too this" and "you're too that." You're sensitive, you're quiet, you're stupid, you're unstable. You're too active, too lazy, too restless, too soft, too tough, too aggressive. You're **too much**.

We would be pummeled with **"always"** statements too. You always do what you want, you always do the same thing, you always get distracted, you always make the same mistakes, you're always wrong, you always fail. We were also told that we were "never" doing things that we were supposed to be doing. You never pay attention, you never listen, you never do what you have to do.

We were threatened with the unrelenting prophecy of **"never"** being able to accomplish things either. You'll never pass, you'll never find a job, you'll never have a girlfriend, you'll never be happy, you'll never change, you'll never do what I tell you.

We were beaten with the club of guilt and discouraged with the accusing finger of shame. We grew up in fear of **falling short** or being disrespected.

Our feelings of inadequacy and alienation came up in the classroom, in our offices and in our families. We felt **weird**, strange and ostracized for having different tastes and interests. We felt unwelcome for thinking differently and for unintentionally going against the crowd.

We feel ashamed for having a mental block, being at a loss for words or freezing up in situations that are **stressful** for everyone. We feel guilty after losing a game in sports to an opponent that is better than us, for failing a difficult exam, for not getting chosen after a job interview, for not feeling more love for our partner and for wanting to leave a relationship that is going nowhere.

Every time we feel guilty, we feel that we deserve to be punished for having done something wrong. We regress to our childhood, adolescence or earlier times. Our mind has internalized our teachers, our father, our mother and demanding and authoritarian police officers, and it treats us the same way.

We were **bad** students, bad children, bad siblings, bad partners, bad workers and bad parents. We made mistakes, we failed and we didn't get where we wanted to be. We didn't live up to what was expected of us.

Therefore, we are not **worthy** of being loved or receiving affection. We deserve our suffering. We deserve to be punished and shamed. And in some places in the world, we were told that if we do not meet the cultural expectations of those in power, then we deserve to be whipped, tortured and stoned. Shame is the echo of others' mockery; guilt is our well-deserved reprimand from authority.

Guilt is a result of bullying by individuals or groups, of constant demands, of the ideal of perfection and of the illusion of control. Guilt is the cause of most psychological disorders (or it plays a supporting role). Parents, teachers, bosses and any person or entity in power all play on this feeling that we deserve punishment to hook us in, win our loyalty, trap us and hold their **moral** judgment over us.

They fail us and pass us, reward us and punish us, directly or by comparison.

Favorite children, model students, employees of the month and exemplary citizens all hide the **seed** of guilt inside, strictly following orders to avoid feelings of alienation.

Guilt is **addictive**. It comes to us from birth, just as it has been with humanity since the development of language and identity. When it vanishes or its expression peters off to a minimum, an uncomfortable **emptiness** appears, giving rise to the idea that we are letting down our parents, our family, our religion, our society or our culture.

A client asked me, "Why don't I feel bad that I've stopped working?"

The **virus** of guilt rattles the *replicative* mind, making it snap to attention and motivating it to bring out its best version. Guilt separates and twists the *evolutive* mind, shutting it down and blocking it from being itself.

The worst **version** of guilt arises simply from feeling or thinking something. This is the guilt that rules our inner world with an iron fist. It is a feeling that sticks to everything instinctive and natural that is automatically activated—everything that happens inside us but is not truly ours.

Guilt draws on the **past**, which is over and done. "You shouldn't have done that." "If only you had thought about that first." "I told you not to do that." "If only I had done this instead of that." It fixates on what could never have been different and on what cannot be changed.

All this absurd guilt overwhelms us and punishes us constantly. The ultimate emotional trap is to feel guilty for feeling guilty. We walk on eggshells, balancing on a tightrope and dodging hornet nests. And it's all due to excessive guilt. We even feel guilty for growing older and aging.

Guilt is as harsh as the tone of the histrionic mother or the authoritarian teacher we had. It is **simplistic** because it reduces a mistake to an isolated act, ignoring the influence of all other factors. It is **unmindful** because it does not take into account the influence of the context and other people involved.

It is **shortsighted** because it ignores the previous and complex chain of causes and effects that culminated in the unfortunate result. It is **unfair** because it singles us out and attacks our entire personality for a mistake. It is **sadistic** because it is more interested in punishment and humiliation than in dignity and reparation.

Did you distrust him because you're unfair or because he'd lied to you before? Did you shout at him because you're mean, or did he shout at you first? Did you end the relationship because you wanted to or because it was inevitable?

"But I'm guilty of not knowing how to communicate." And how do your parents communicate with you and with each other? Did they teach you emotional communication? What if that's another skill to learn? And most of all, do you realize that, considering the parents you had and the upbringing they gave you, you're not so bad at it either?

The **illusion** that everything depends on us and that each of us is our own isolated cause, the origin and beginning of everything that happens to us, is an attractive and tempting idea. It sends us on a quest for the starting point, the clean slate, the original beginning. Outwardly, we appear confident and free, yet inwardly, we feel bitterly **lonely**.

In reality, nothing starts from scratch, not even birth itself. Relationships are shaped by previous relationships, jobs by previous jobs. Everything has a precedent, a consequence of a consequence, which gives us these tendencies, temperaments, scars and lessons learned. The illusion of **reinvention** does so much damage!

Freedom of action is based on the illusion that we have freedom of thought, since for mainstream psychology, action is a consequence of a previous thought, which is the cause of it. This is the rational logic of the top-down or the higher pathway.

According to mainstream messaging, you must first imagine something in your head, then desire it with all your might so that it may magically materialize, because *the whole universe is on your side.*

The **illusion** that we always choose our feelings, tastes and desires is assumed to be true. In the same way, we are supposed to continually **decide** on our beliefs, thoughts and judgments.

And since we **control** our body and mind, we are free to choose what we want. Therefore, anyone who has unpleasant emotions or difficult thoughts or who makes complicated decisions is exercising their own free will. Or it's their fault for having or making them. In the end, it's the same thing.

Because "if you want to do it, you can," and "if they could do it, so can you." Because "the world is yours," "you are free to do whatever you want," and "with hard work and dedication and by believing in yourself, you can achieve whatever you set your mind to."

You were free to choose option A and you chose B. No one forced you into that situation, and you deserve to deal with the consequences of your mistake. And since you decided to lose yourself, it's up to you to find yourself. *Because we are all born with the same opportunities and the same abilities. There is abundance for everyone.*

I don't remember exactly when in my childhood I crawled into the personality store and chose the one

I have. And I don't remember asking Santa Claus for what kind of childhood I wanted to have. I also don't remember when my nervous system, with its sympathetic tendency toward cortisol and stress, a gift from my mother, was surgically removed and replaced with a better one, with a parasympathetic tendency toward calmness and oxytocin.

"Don't judge! Stop judging!" the last mainstream psychologist I saw told me. As she scolded me, she was unaware that she was judging my own judgment. Her constructive criticism only confused me more, and I left her office feeling guiltier than when I had arrived, this time for not knowing how to do something as simple as stopping judging.

Most mainstream psychologists don't know that many thoughts think themselves and that a majority of our judgments are self-made. They believe that everything that happens in our minds, and the ideas that we are aware of, belong to us and are intentional, and that we have deliberately created these thoughts.

First it was **religion**, then academic psychology. At first it was our parents, then the gurus who blamed us for having feelings and thoughts. "The quality of your life depends on the quality of your thoughts." "Happiness is a matter of attitude." "Everything is a matter of attitude."

"You are the architect of your destiny and the creator of your own reality," prophesied guilt, dressed up in New Age grandiloquence. This leads to so much confusion and future frustration disguised as motivation and good intentions.

The idea of freedom applied to psychology plants a seed of emotional discomfort. If you don't have the ideal job, partner, body, image or life, it's because you don't really want it or you're not trying hard enough. If we were free, we would all choose to be intelligent, enthusiastic, strong, invulnerable, rich, beautiful and successful.

The tried-and-true techniques, the meditation workshops and relaxation retreats, the doctors and psychologists—we assume that they are infallible, that they would never be wrong. If the medication that works for one person doesn't work for you, if journaling doesn't fit your lifestyle or if yoga doesn't help clear your mind, that's your own fault.

Today, you can decide to quit your job and change careers. Tomorrow, you could lie on the couch all day. The day after tomorrow, you could start drinking beer instead of water. Experience your **illusion of freedom** firsthand. Realize that even if you love fairy tales, fairies don't really exist. Mainstream culture promotes **anti-values** based on fear, guilt and envy. It promotes superficiality because it is shortsighted and hurried. These principles are easier to manipulate.

As a result, we strive for ostentation, vanity, fame, success, positive appearances, money, business, a nice body, a desirable partner, competitiveness, work, effort, sacrifice and happiness.

IT SEEMS THAT HAVING A PARTNER, CHILDREN, MONEY, A BODY OR A LIFE THAT OTHERS ENVY ARE THE ONLY GOALS FOR MOST PEOPLE.

Our **conscience** springs from guilt. Without conflict, there is no guilt. You can't have a conscience without a certain degree of intelligence, and you can't have **real intelligence** without a certain degree of sensitivity. If you say that you had a happy childhood, it wouldn't be a stretch to say that you don't have too much of a conscience because you haven't felt guilt.

However, once our conscience expands, guilt no longer makes sense as a code of conduct, just as the feeling of guilt traced the red line of proper morality in times before civil or penal codes. With conscience, there are values, and we no longer need guilt to control our behavior.

Once conscience unfolds within us and we become aware of the causes and consequences of our actions, we can discern what is right or wrong, useful or useless, productive or unproductive, and appropriate or inappropriate according to each situation.

To continue evolving, we must gradually wean ourselves from this mainstream addiction to self-flagellation and build our own ethics and values to navigate through life. Guilt becomes useless, like a dog barking at a wall.

Thoughts and feelings are not a reliable **compass** either. We cannot entrust our lives to something as intense and ever-changing as these two unconscious phenomena. We must listen to them, but we cannot build our lives on the unstable shifting sands of the mind and body.

We also can't let our nervous system take control and call all the shots in our lives. As a tool for survival, it's fantastic, but as a mechanism for growth, it has its drawbacks. If we always did what our nervous system told us, we would regret the outcomes and reinforce the idea that reason (which is blamed) is the only reliable decision-making center.

Our nervous system, thoughts and emotions change. Values and principles remain stable, and are necessary on our journey. The first three concepts are the tracks along which the train glides. Our values and principles are the overhead power cable that gives the train energy and movement.

The mind and body are wonderful and surprising, and they often get things right. Yet by their very nature, they are also imprecise, fluctuating and erratic, without necessarily being wrong. However, what is important (my principles) is nonnegotiable and must **guide** my life.

I don't know if I see anything with full clarity. But I can make out a path, a kind of escalator that keeps moving forward "despite" and "through" my fears and insecurities. It stretches out before me, even though I'm sometimes harried with **doubt**. When what's important guides my steps, my nervous system trusts the overhead power cable and learns to flow more with life.

Slowly, the *lower pathway* (my nervous system, feelings and thoughts) is reconciled with the *upper pathway* (values, the spiritual part). That's when I trust in life. After all, it is life that has created my nervous system and therefore chosen my values.

We must learn to align our **instincts** with our values. We must pivot from the belief that "the more I suffer, the more I punish myself," reinforcing guilt as a moral and behavioral **code**, to "the more I suffer, the more I must try to care for myself," focusing on our values to guide us toward a virtuous life.

If I feel tired, frustrated, sad or low on energy, I am kind to myself and engage in activities that help me feel as good as possible, soothe me and treat me with care and dignity.

It is important to do things to *connect* with our principles rather than to do them to **avoid** feeling guilty. I don't give treats to my dog, Víctor, because I feel bad (guilty) about the long car ride. I give him treats to celebrate the principle of **justice**. He deserves it. He has made driving easier on me and has made spending all day on the road less tiresome.

I can also visit my grandmother more often because I see that her health is deteriorating and I love her (values), or I can visit her to avoid feeling guilty when she eventually passes away. We see how the same action can conceal opposing motivations. From the perspective of values, we would experience it with a sense of choice, freedom and growth. From the perspective of guilt, we would experience it with a sense of sorrow, duty and implicit bitterness.

A guy tries to trip me on the subway. I can ignore him, ask him why he did that, tell him off or shove him. I can ignore him to avoid shoving him, so I don't feel guilty, or I can ignore him because he's got a screw loose and I don't believe in violence (values).

I can ask him why he did that so he can see that it's wrong and understand his actions (values), or I can confront him to avoid feeling like a wimp, like when I was bullied in school (guilt). I can shove him because I think it's the fairest thing to do so he can learn not to try to trip others (justice, values, the **common good**), or I can do it to avoid feeling like a coward for leaving without confronting my aggressor (once again, guilt).

I can respond to his aggression so he can learn, or I can do the same and feel bad. I can refrain from shoving him because I believe in peace, or I can hold back to avoid feeling bad and guilty later. The same action can diminish us (guilt) or make us **grow** (principles).

According to mainstream moralists, we are capable of doing both good and terrible things, and both extremes may contain wonderful values of love, respect, justice and kindness.

The same values have different meanings and actions associated with them, depending on the person.

It's healthy to challenge yourself and cross the boundaries of mainstream principles, letting yourself feel. **Allow yourself** to feel anger, sadness, fear, guilt and shame. Continue stretching the mainstream mold a little until you feel more comfortable with your actions and your life.

Your life is not your own until you are comfortable with your **own** values, felt by your body and conceptualized by your mind after being experienced.

Values undergo transformation (and can even come into opposition) based on whether we have *replicative* or *evolutive* tendencies. For some, keeping a wild animal in captivity is a form of care and protection; for others, it is an awful type of mistreatment. The depth of someone's perspective and the level of their analysis defines their **intention**.

I try to live my life based on my principles of awareness, sensitivity, **imperfection** and weirdness, and not from a place of fear, obligation or guilt. This kind of life includes anger, sadness, fear and obviously joy. It has its share of mistakes *and* achievements.

However, acting like I am perfect and crowing about my success would be the worst message I could send to a society fragmented by envy and ostentation.

When I can, I like to add value to my community. Sometimes I get into trouble or take risks to raise awareness or transform situations. I like to review products on Amazon and establishments on Google Maps, regardless of whether the reviews I leave are good or bad.

I feel that there is widespread tolerance for corporations to deceive and mistreat their clients, customers and consumers. I'm motivated by feelings of justice, respect and the **common good**.

My brother, who is a *replicant*, considers my bad reviews to be absurdly **unfair**, whereas I see them as acts of love, commitment and beauty. We came out of the same womb thirteen months apart, and we couldn't be less alike.

My brother never broke a plate; I smashed the dishes. He's rather cautious and fearful; I'm bolder and can be more reckless. He stays on the shore; I swim to the buoy. He can't be me, and I can't be him. We respect each other's **personalities** and associated roles.

What are you going to do if your neighbor likes to set off firecrackers at three in the morning? Whether he's "sane" or has a certified mental disorder, are you going to keep quiet? Are you going to allow it? Are you going to try to "set things straight"?

It doesn't depend entirely on you, but rather, on your nervous system. Some keep quiet and suffer in silence. Others adapt, then compensate. Still others of us confront each other, trying to resolve conflicts for our own well-being and that of the community. Is a **fair**, justified and proportional amount of **aggression** always immoral?

My nervous system is well-tuned. It abhors injustice, and I won't be able to change that. I've tried countless times to turn a blind eye to situations that feel wrong to me, always with the same results: more repression, tension, restraint, explosion and again, more guilt. I can try to deal with external causes and stop trying to change what we can't.

I can also leave and seek a connection with other like-minded sensitive people. In these cases, however, I shouldn't question whether my nervous system is attuned and in sync. In general, it doesn't become hyperactivated on a whim, but rather, as a result of injustice. It strives for the truth, seeking to avoid the overwhelming feeling of loneliness.

On an emotional level, I stopped feeling guilty for who I am when I removed the thorns stuck in my side (the *biographical burden*). Those included all the situations I went through in childhood, my teenage years and early adulthood that had left their mark on me, making me feel inadequate, alone, rejected, abandoned or traumatized.

On a **cognitive level**, I stopped feeling guilty when I erased the word "guilt" from my vocabulary.

On a **behavioral level**, I stopped feeling guilty when I started living my life according to my own values and ethical principles.

On a **relational level**, I stopped feeling guilty when I stopped making others feel guilty for not measuring up to what I expected them to be or do.

On a **spiritual level**, I stopped feeling guilty when I understood the absurdity of the message of freedom spread by mainstream culture.

Any social lobby (whether linked to religion, politics, psychology or the media) that tries to make us feel guilty or afraid aims to send us back to a past where we had to submit to the will of others to survive. **Being held in captivity** is not a value; it is a punishment from which we can escape.

As children, we didn't talk enough about values at the family dinner table or in the classroom with our teachers. Your father was your hero until you saw his mask slip. Your mother was a saint until you caught her cursing. Your teachers disappointed you because they extolled ideals without setting an example.

When *evolutive* people grow to adulthood, they are unlikely to continue to look to their parents as **role models**. Their family has blamed these evolutive people, and they end up searching for the solution elsewhere, by experiencing life: trying new things, traveling and mingling with a world that eludes them.

We are the books we read, the people we listen to, the movies we see and the media we watch and follow. We are what attracts us, and attraction is not a choice. Role models reveal your hidden sides. Tell me who you follow and who you admire, and I'll tell you who you are.

If you admire tormented people, you are (or have been) tormented. If you admire people who appear perfect, guilt consumes you from within for not being perfect as well, and you pretend to be like them. If you admire relatable and natural people, sooner or later you'll let yourself be who you are. You'll be at peace with yourself and shed your feelings of guilt.

Henry Rollins was like a father to me. I met him when I was eighteen after reading an article in a rock music magazine. I was struck by his stature, his penetrating gaze, his tattoos and his short, side-parted hair in a music scene where most people wore their hair long. He didn't drink, he didn't smoke, he read Kafka and Nietzsche, and he played chess. He spoke his mind and had brilliant insights.

I bought all his CDs and several of his books in English. His music was pure aggression and allowed me to vent my anger and frustration. His introspective and profound lyrics gave words to my pain living in the world of adults. I covered the walls of my room with his posters, joined the gym and adopted his influences as my own.

That same year, I met him when he came to Barcelona for a concert. In the concert hall, I felt euphoric, ecstatic and full of adrenaline. It was an unprecedented experience of art, violence and intensity for me.

After the concert, I waited for him outside to ask him for his autograph. I was speechless when I saw him come out. I touched his shoulder, and it seemed like he was made of stone. Up close, he acted reserved and aloof. He signed a poster for me, and I went home feeling both enlightened and nostalgic.

He was the first famous person I'd seen open up in public. He revealed his childhood secrets in detail, speaking frankly about his obsessions and insecurities, baring his soul. "I see the truth as my shield. As long as I tell the truth, I feel that nobody can touch me."

Maybe it was with Henry that the brew of **REAL psychology** began to simmer. To be REAL is to speak from who we are, not from who we would like to be. It's about showing ourselves as we are, not how we wish others would see us. And it's about doing so with **dignity** and **without guilt** or **shame**.

The purpose of our role models is to expand our options and offer us new **possibilities**. They light up new paths, showing us the whole spectrum of hues. They show us new roles, hidden corners and latent parts of ourselves that allow us to discover things we share with others.

Role models help us put words to our mental blocks. They help us identify, value and learn from our blind spots. They help us understand our personal challenges as normal. They lighten our burdens of guilt and shame through cathartic liberation from certain difficult parts of our own life story or of our personality.

We feel more **understood**, safer and less alone when we feel connected to someone we admire. They embellish the mediocre, making the world less monotonous and ugly.

Through role models, we test out and distill our own body of values, building a new belief system. They help us leave our family guilt behind. We discover new tastes, tendencies, desires, talents and dilemmas. We cross to the other side of the river of tradition. We see what we are made of. Their art and their message soothe the form (the body) and complete the foundation (the soul).

True role models don't diminish us or elicit envy in us. They don't blame or manipulate us. They infuse us with authenticity, creative energy and vitality. They inspire us without pushing us and coax us without coercing us. They make things easier on us, lightening our load and lifting us up. They stir and animate us to be more authentic, to dare to express more of who we are.

We are drawn to role models because our guilt temporarily evaporates in their presence, giving rise to a sense of meaning and freedom. Their story moves us. We identify with their biography. They awaken our talents, making us create, believe and dream. They provide new solutions to old problems.

They don't point out our shortcomings but shine light on our **talents**. They don't put themselves above us, and they don't clamber onto our shoulders to appear gigantic. They help us grow, create and build.

They **validate** our experience. Their journey accompanies our own. Deep down, we feel that they understand us because they have been through the same thing. From a distance, they seem more relatable to us than many of our relatives and more generous than many of our friends.

Just as the **lighthouse** does not blind the boat with its glare, role models only light a path toward the harbor. They let us evolve, guiding us toward what is REAL. To do so, they show themselves as they truly are, with their contradictions and insecurities, full of weirdness and humanity.

They fill the **emotional voids** left by parents and family members. When we feel disoriented, they step into our minds. This is even more the case if mainstream morality has discombobulated us or if its absence has left us stranded in the desert.

The people we admire speak publicly about what they really feel, with no fillers or sweeteners. They help us be at **peace** with ourselves. They help us understand the difficult thoughts that mainstream culture has blamed as natural.

They are humble and downplay their importance. They recognize the role that luck has played in what they've accomplished and the factors that have influenced their achievements.

If we lack role models, we end up reluctantly following in our family's footsteps. We have no other choice but to follow the tradition of our upbringing, which sets the acceptable **standards**, path and mindset. Unless you are living your life in mode 1 (Chapter 1), you will endure the demotivation of your inner circle and the creative stagnation and inauthenticity pushed by the representatives of mainstream culture.

Without role models, we drift aimlessly, following the dull, monotonous and **senseless** rhythms of mainstream culture. If we don't have role models, they will be imposed on us, because we are bereft of connection and meaning, which is their purpose. We all have role models. Some of them we are aware of, and we align them with our lives, while others are unconscious and assigned to us by popular culture. These false role models make us feel like we belong at the cost of feeling empty or manipulated.

False role models assume a position of superiority over you, ostentatiously posing as divine figures, creating psychologically distant, dependent and condescending relationships and abusing the false power you've granted them. False role models are impostors, swindlers and liars.

We do not choose our role models willingly. The connection is unforced and happens naturally. A spontaneous tuning takes place between two nervous systems. Two stories, one of the artist and one of the follower, become intertwined. The work of art and the viewer become as one. It is an organic communion. It is just like when a plug fits into an outlet and the light turns on.

WEIRDNESS ATTRACTS WEIRDNESS LIKE INTELLIGENCE ATTRACTS INTELLIGENCE, LIKE SENSITIVITY ATTRACTS SENSITIVITY, LIKE CREATIVITY ATTRACTS CREATIVITY AND LIKE BEAUTY ATTRACTS BEAUTY.

Suddenly, a role model appears in your life, and the answer appears. Your questioning stops, the nonsense fades, you glimpse a way out of the maze, and a weight is lifted.

An anonymous but intimate relationship is established. It turns into a mental image that shapes you, helping you out of difficult situations and accompanying you everywhere. You have a new **home**. You are no longer an orphan and no longer walk alone. Their path is your path, though with different landscapes and forks along the way.

When a role model dies, so does something deep inside you. You grieve, just like when a family member or a loved one dies.

Through their message, their art and their example, we have experienced more hope, understanding and inspiration than with most people we have met in person. They have come along on many of our adventures and misadventures and have been there in many of our positive and negative interactions. We remove the stigma of guilt with them and feel the **beauty of our weirdness** for the first time.

When a role model of mine passes away, I go back to their books, their music, their photos, their letters and their messages, and I allow myself to feel the sadness and the nostalgia. They still have something to teach me, even after death. Everything ends, and nothing lasts forever. It's just that they leave first.

My personal role models taught me to speak, to think, to write, to sing, to play the guitar, to walk, to make friends, to manage my emotions, to dream, to travel, to love my weirdness, to soften my guilt and to find my own way.

Most have been rock singers, writers, actors, musicians, entrepreneurs, adventurers and athletes. They have been creative, charismatic, controversial, transgressive, **weird** and special beings without forcing anything or being histrionic. They have been people who did not set out to make a mark, yet stand out in some way for their **strength and conviction**, or for their sensitivity and depth, or for their intelligence, or their bravery.

They have been people who had it tough and swam against the current, ahead of their time. It was this outside opposition that paved the way for us, broadened our horizons and made room for the rest of us. Thanks to them, we embrace more of our own weirdness, as we saw it in them first. It is because of them that we are more ourselves today.

The most **beautiful** message I receive from my readers, clients and followers on social media is that they feel less guilty and allow themselves to be themselves more. Through my example, they live with more clarity and make fewer mistakes. They feel lighter by being more REAL.

Freedom

Man can do what he wills, but
he cannot will what he wills.

Arthur Schopenhauer

Today is a great day. Starting today, all your dreams will come true. You'll see that you can do anything you set your mind to. You just have to **think big** and claim your birthright. You have to want it badly enough. We were all born to be happy and to live in peace and abundance. If you don't achieve that, it's because you don't yet believe that you deserve it enough. If you fail, it's because you're doing something wrong. Everything depends on you; it's your **choice** whether to succeed or fail.

Mario is **free**. He has realized this, so starting today, he's going to **decide** to do whatever he wants because he is free.

He can choose to sleep for as many hours as he wants, and he'll still get enough rest. Why not sleep nine and a half hours straight? He's going to cut his hair however he wants without caring what others think. He's going to work twelve hours in a row without getting exhausted. He's heterosexual, but today he's going to be attracted to men and have his first fling. He's going to win the lottery jackpot and go vegan.

María is **free**. She has realized this, and has decided to grow four inches. She's going to change the color of her eyes. She's going to get pregnant and find the cure for cancer. She's going to stay up all night and sleep during the day. She's going to go live alone. She's going to stop eating and live off air. She's going to fall madly in love with someone, and she's going to win at bingo.

How many people want to be rich, and how many achieve it? How many people want financial freedom, and how many accomplish it? How many people want a stunning natural body, and how many get it? How many people want to be happy in a relationship, and how many succeed at it? And what does it mean to be rich? What does financial freedom mean? What does it mean to have an attractive body? And what does happiness mean? And happiness in a relationship? What does it all mean? Is there a single, general, universal definition applicable for everyone? Does everything mean the same thing to everyone?

It's psychologically healthy to aspire to beautiful things and to improve our current situation. However, if those dreams don't match our talents, tendencies and limitations, they will turn into nightmares. Life will be an endless hill to climb, a Sisyphean effort where despite our best efforts to ascend one step, we end up going down two. And wherever we go, we will wear the albatross of guilt and shame around our neck.

Freedom is the natural ability to act or not act in one way or another, while being responsible for our actions. Freedom means not being subject or subordinate to anything or anyone. Freedom is a value that ensures people's **free determination**.

Freedom is a **fundamental right** of civilized human beings in a democratic system. It's the ability to do what is permitted by law, as long as it doesn't harm others. Furthermore, fundamental rights (human rights) legally guarantee us the freedom to shape and express our personality without state interference.

Therefore, we all have freedom of thought and **ideology**; freedom of expression and opinion; freedom of conscience, creed, worship and religion; freedom of information and education; freedom of commerce and consumption; freedom of association, business and union; and freedom to private life and movement.

I've informally surveyed about two hundred native Romance language speakers, including clients, family members, friends, acquaintances and strangers, about the meaning of freedom or **being free**. For most, freedom means "doing whatever I want" or "not having anyone tell me what to do." For others, freedom means having enough money to not worry about it or to afford certain advantages.

It can also mean enjoying free time or being in control of your schedule. It can mean being able to shop or travel whenever you want, enjoying flexible working hours or being able to work remotely (freedom of location or being a digital nomad). It can mean having sexual freedom or freedom in your type of romantic or loving relationship (closed or open, monogamous or polyamorous). For others, freedom means not having anxiety and being able to breathe calmly.

Young people confuse wanting with being able to. They conflate a **desire** (often created and mediated by mainstream culture) with a possibility, an idea with a fact and a thought with a situation. Young people are more idealistic, inexperienced, enthusiastic and vulnerable to the mercantilist idea of freedom and the notion that life is a carte blanche.

Younger people are the ones who suffer the most from the **entrapment** of mainstream culture. They are more vulnerable to the basic and primary concept of freedom, of "doing whatever I want." Basically, they associate freedom with giving free rein to the basic drives of their nervous system. They also have a simplified concept of freedom linked to autonomy of action or movement, of "going wherever I want whenever I want."

For older *replicative* people, the idea of freedom is connected to superficial mainstream values, such as financial freedom or professional autonomy.

However, for former inmates, freedom means not being deprived of it. Great figures of humanity such as Viktor Frankl, Nelson Mandela, José Mujica and Mario Conde said that they had never been freer than in prison. There, they enjoyed an **inner freedom** they had never experienced before. They studied and wrote freely, compelled by a sense of belonging to a greater cause that sublimated their central personal desire for freedom. For them, it was the triumph of the superior freedom of their moral and spiritual principles over the deprivation of primary freedom, the freedom of movement.

Furthermore, there are more conservative cultures based on old traditions and religions, and there are more progressive cultures based on values and democracy. In traditional cultures, there is more repression and censorship; in progressive cultures, there is initially less. In progressive cultures, the consumer society offers people more options. Therefore, they enjoy a greater perception of freedom, whether aesthetic or consumer-oriented (more television channels, more presumed options for finding a partner and so on).

Freedom is a tricky concept. Some feel liberated when they break the rules, shirk their responsibilities or ignore instructions. Yet for others, that feels like being led by their passions. For some, freedom means escaping obligations, while to others, it means honoring them, even if they don't feel like it sometimes.

On a deeper **level of analysis**, only by following the rules can we enjoy the true "feeling" of freedom. Just as the waters of a river flow freely because they follow their course, we drive safely because we obey traffic signs.

Therefore, depending on the situation, freedom cannot exist without obligations to meet, and our instincts can lead us to the brink of temptation.

Similarly, some people feel free by being their own boss, keeping their own hours, with the ability to earn more and to choose how they do so. Others feel that freedom in the opposite way: by having a fixed salary, following a schedule and knowing where they will be at all times.

SOME PEOPLE FIND FREEDOM BY FOLLOWING A SECURE PATH, AND OTHERS DO SO BY LEAVING THE SAFETY OF THE HARBOR.

Some people associate freedom with **following their heart**. Others associate it with **resisting emotional urges** and acting according to their values. For some, freedom is the rule of reason, reflection and philosophy; for others, it is the realm of feeling, fantasy and imagination.

Some people tend to conform and submit from birth, while others tend to rebel and resist. Both can find comfort, but they do so by going in opposite directions. The quickest route to freedom is to act as you truly are. *Evolutive* people rebel, and *replicative* people conform. Both are as they are.

An animal born and raised in captivity feels free in a cage as an adult. It is a matter of time before most nervous systems adapt to their circumstances and begin to feel at home in them. The drug addict thinks he is free because he takes his dose wherever and whenever he wants. The homeless man prefers a cold night alone to a warm shelter full of rules.

The concept of freedom depends on **context**: situation, culture, values, age, gender and personality. Therefore, it is a relative, biased and not very "free" term in itself. It is another magic concept that mainstream culture uses to dazzle and distract us with the promise of perfection and the punishment of guilt.

Freedom is a vague and conventionally imposed idea. We take it for granted and rarely question it individually. If our nervous system has decided our tendencies and preferences for us, and mainstream culture has dictated our rights and duties, are we truly free? Maybe we aren't physiologically or culturally free, though psychologically we need that healthy **illusion** to function at our best. It's also crucial to understand the different levels of freedom and learn how to manage them so we don't become followers of the religion of guilt.

You can order whatever you want off the menu. Are you free to eat whatever you want? If the options have been determined in advance, **are we really free**?

Mammals are driven by their instincts to protect, survive and socialize. They live freely in nature, but are equally vulnerable to its dangers, other predators and harsh weather. Dogs are bound to their instincts, but they live safely in captivity, deprived of their freedom. Why is freedom often considered a higher value than **security**?

Do we become happier with more freedom? Are we happier as we get more money and free time? Is freedom a direct path to happiness? Will we always feel better to the extent that we enjoy more freedom?

Why do they want us to believe that freedom and happiness are synonymous and positively correlated? Who benefits from this?

What is your favorite color? And your favorite food?

Your favorite genre of music? What type of woman or man attracts you sexually?

Can you **choose** when to be hungry, when to be thirsty, when to go to sleep, when to make a lifelong friend or when to fall in love? Did I **decide** that I don't like onions and that I hate local festivals?

Do you remember choosing your temperament, your IQ, your EQ, your degree of sensitivity or introversion, the childhood traumas you experienced or your mother and father's parenting style? Did you choose to be heterosexual or bisexual? Did you choose your gender fluidity?

Did you choose the country where you were born? The religion that informed and shaped your culture and traditions?

Right now, your whole life is a **result** of and is dependent on all the intangible and invisible things that you didn't choose, but make you who you are.

Right here, right now.

Most people have fallen for the **trap** of freedom and are convinced that they have chosen their hobbies, talents and limitations. Deep down, they feel a lot of guilt.

I didn't choose to like rock music. Somehow, it chose me.

One summer night, when I was fourteen, I was sitting

on the balcony at home, wearing headphones, when I heard a guitar riff by the Cult.

I suddenly felt relief, with a light and tingling sensation of simple clarity. I felt my stomach, my heart, my lungs and my jaw open and expand. Some internal knots came loose, and I found peace.

The images that appeared in my head were full of faith, joy, hope and enthusiasm. My shame was transformed into confidence. The plug had fit into the outlet, and the light had switched on.

I listened to the tape several times that night. My pleasure was so great and the **therapeutic effect** was so revelatory that my nervous system craved it more and more. And we're still repeating it today.

I never stopped listening to rock. It was the soundtrack of my turbulent teenage years and my youth. Its aggressive sound gave me a tribe, an aesthetic and a culture alongside the mainstream one.

A new world opened up while on my balcony that night, simply through a guitar riff. And it happened suddenly, with no planning involved.

I didn't choose to like **tattoos**. Tattoos chose me.

When I was a teenager, the walls of my room were plastered with rock band posters. All the musicians had tattoos. Out of admiration, imitation and a sense of belonging, I ended up getting tattoos as an adult.

We become our role models. It's as simple as that.

I didn't choose to be a **psychologist**. Being a psychologist chose me.

I got fed up with studying psychology. I didn't believe in academic psychology. After I completed my formal studies, I knew I would never practice.

Three years later, I moved to California, where I became deeply involved in various spiritual practices and other types of psychotherapy.

Then I returned to Barcelona. Seven years later, I opened my psychology practice with no sense of pressure.

I didn't choose to be a **writer**. Being a writer chose me.

I was always a voracious reader and good at writing down my thoughts, stories and poems. Everywhere I went, I carried my pen and notebook, taking notes on everything. I tried to get my writing published, but nobody gave me a chance.

Five years after I had given up on writing and begun my career as a psychologist, a publisher suggested that I compile my thoughts in my first book, *Manual de espiritualidad rebelde.*

It didn't happen when I wanted it to. It happened after I'd already thrown in the towel.

These are only four examples, but they show that this is how life works. I have dozens of stories that only further confirm that I never decided on most of the important things I've experienced in life. They simply happened. And they often happened while I was living my life, not lying on the couch at home.

Our choices, selections and decision-making come more from our **gut** than we think. They depend less on our will and precede reason more than we would like to believe.

In reality, they **surge** up immediately from within. Our choices simply happen, just like that, and by feeling, observing and mentally analyzing them in our body, we believe we have triggered them with our rational mind.

In this way, we reinforce the **mirage** of freedom, viewing **this natural and organic process** upside down and making it appear more top-down or rational than it really is.

The tree grows from the roots to the branches, and not the other way around. The present moment emerges from the past, and not the other way around. Adulthood follows childhood, and not the other way around. Reason and feeling come from the nervous system, and not the other way around.

The **transformation inherent** in life moves forward and upward. Theoretically, any change is possible and has its place, but it will only come when the time is right. It will only happen when several different causes and conditions make it possible.

What happens in my head is one thing, and what happens in life is another. My thoughts are one thing, and **reality** is another. Sometimes they align, and sometimes they oppose each other.

Five monkeys decide to leap from a branch into a pond. How many monkeys are left on the branch? All five decided to jump, but not all of them actually did so. Wanting something is never the same as being able to do it, though sometimes the two can overlap.

I can decide to go eat at an Italian restaurant instead of a Japanese restaurant and end up at a Lebanese restaurant. The Italian restaurant was closed and the Japanese restaurant was full. Life always takes precedence over the mind.

CONTROL IS A FANTASY AND A LOT OF COINCIDENCE.

Once I became aware of this possibility, I thought about it, questioned it and subjected it to trial and error. Nothing has to change completely, but everything can change at the same time.

I just pay a little more attention to where life leads me.

In 2022, I wanted to leave the apartment I had started renting in Barcelona in 2021. I was sick of the city. I felt glum and bored. I compared different options for months and sought out information about different regions, cities and countries. Nothing seemed quite right.

A sudden, casual conversation with someone I barely knew set me on the path of my new destination.

I got the message and moved there in late 2022, convinced that it was time to move away for a while to a town I had never heard of before.

One day in the spring of 2023, images of summer appeared in my mind. I sensed I would spend July in Stockholm and that in August I would travel across northern Spain, avoiding staying in a city no matter what and especially getting away from the heat of Barcelona.

I hate the subtropical Spanish heat, and the official holiday season is the worst time of year for me. It's extremely hot, places are overcrowded, and prices are through the roof.

In the end, I spent July in Stockholm, but nothing

was free in the cooler part of Spain in August, and I had to stay in stifling Barcelona.

I didn't like it, but I didn't fight against my **fate**. It came easily. I didn't feel like it, but it was the best thing for me.

In the end, we always end up going where we're supposed to. We go where we're invited or where we're pushed if we resist. We go where we knock and the door opens. We go where we're welcomed.

Mainstream culture teaches us to work hard, sacrifice and let ourselves be shaped by the traditional education system first, then by the job market. It's hard to break free from this **cultural entrapment**, especially if we're not financially independent.

However, once we hit our thirties, we need to blow off all this outside pressure and take a break. We must learn to know ourselves, understand ourselves, observe ourselves and **choose** the options that best fit our natural way of **being**.

Lightness is sustainable and takes us further.

Many beautiful and important things in my life have happened suddenly, without me having to do much. They happened just by me going out, chatting, sharing, listening, observing, receiving, waiting and letting time **pass**.

They have even happened when I was trying to do something else—when I was focused solely on my next decision or the following step to take.

They say that **man proposes and life disposes**. No matter how much the mind might imagine something, life always decides whether to grant it or not.

Letting ourselves get swept along by events is no **guarantee** that the outcome will be either comfortable or beautiful. However, it is the **best antidote** against analysis paralysis and the futility of mental rumination.

When in doubt, I go where doors open and let life decide through events and specific situations. In this way, my mind breaks out of the loop, and I return to the flow of life.

Sometimes, the truth hurts, but it can't be wrong. It compels us.

One Saturday morning, I woke up wondering whether I should exercise or go for a swim in the ocean after I ate breakfast and walked Víctor. I still wasn't sure when I locked the front door and realized that I'd left my keys inside. I didn't have my phone or my wallet either.

I had just recently moved into a new apartment, and I still hadn't settled into a routine.

I had to go to my aunt's house to get a spare set of keys. I walked four miles uphill that morning. I didn't have breakfast, exercise or swim in the ocean.

The day I had previously imagined had changed **radically**, though I learned two lessons: the importance of making sure that I had my keys before leaving home and the need to know how to **adapt** to the situation in front of me, not the one I had thought I was going to have.

Events take precedence over ideas. Understanding this involves letting go of self-reproach, guilt and especially the harmful illusion of freedom.

What would have happened if my aunt had gone away for the weekend? What would I have done without my phone, keys, money or ID? How would the situation have been resolved?

There is a popular Indian saying that goes like this: "Believe in God, pray to God, but when you leave home, lock your door twice."

Acceptance

Chance plays by very cruel rules. If you understand the rules, you accept life better.

Commonly attributed to Arturo Pérez-Reverte

"Acceptance" is another magic concept and therefore another bait and switch. The government uses it to calm people down when things go wrong, religion uses it to convince the faithful, and false gurus use it to abuse those who follow their programs. We also use it because it's fashionable and sounds powerful or because we don't know what else to say or do. "That's just how it goes," we say. "You've got to accept it."

We also use it to shirk responsibility and to avoid getting upset. "Just deal with it," we say. "You have to accept it."

The meaning of acceptance and its mechanics are generally unknown. Accepting something is mistaken for liking something, or it's believed to be a simple mental process, like pressing a button: something that either happens right away or doesn't happen at all. People also think that acceptance takes the form of a syllogism or a mathematical calculation and requires rational effort.

However, acceptance is a process that plays out over **different stages**. It is a gradual succession, divided into phases. We can accept something rationally, emotionally, somatically or bodily, behaviorally and/or spiritually. You may accept that your father disrespected you on his birthday (rational acceptance) but still feel a knot in your stomach when you remember it (somatic lack of acceptance).

We may accept our **inner world** (how we are) and not accept what lies outside (how others are), and vice versa. I may accept some parts of myself, or all of them, or none at all. The same can happen with other people. We may accept certain aspects of others (when they're nice), but the whole is (always) more complicated.

It's also easier to accept what works for us than what makes us uncomfortable. It's easier to accept when a problem affects someone else than when it blows up in our face.

It also depends on the **context**, the moment, the situation and each person's energy level. For example, if you're well-rested or just had a good meal, you tend to be in a better mood and in higher spirits, and it's easier for you to open up and flow with what life brings your way. However, when you're stressed or under a lot of pressure, you're more likely to clash with, chafe against and resist life's challenges.

Furthermore, because it's fashionable, acceptance is often conflated with other concepts such as submission, resignation or servility, as well as optimism, pacifism or even moral supremacy.

Acceptance is also subject to our personality and our nervous system. Some people have a greater natural tendency toward openness, flexibility and tolerance of the environment. Some find it **easier** to take life as it comes and to adapt to the natural course of events.

However, others (myself included) were born with a **more rigid nervous system**, despite being sensitive, meaning that we can change and be influenced by environmental conditions.

Maybe it was due to the particular circumstances of my development in the womb that my mother's altered nervous system altered my own. Or maybe it was something that was learned as a result of my repressive and unsupportive upbringing. Whatever the case may be, when I was a child, adults (my parents, relatives, teachers and so on) tried to change me through punishment and guilt.

I don't remember anyone accepting my **natural way of being** or applauding me for being myself. Therefore, whether due to temperament or character, my inclination as an adult has been to resist environmental influences so I can remain true to who I am. A cuticle, callus or protective barrier grew around my nervous system to defend my soft and vulnerable side.

As a result, I didn't accept anyone as an adult and tried to change everyone: family members, bosses, friends and girlfriends—with no success, of course. From the blows I had received, I turned myself into a hammer, and I struck back so people would feel the guilt and shame that I had felt before. From the depths of my family's dictatorship, another little dictator emerged. This is common, repeating our family's actions like a broken record. We aren't that original. We learn by **copying and contrasting**, and between these two extremes, we find our own middle ground.

Since I have an *evolutive* mind, I began by copying what I perceived as my father's strict dominance and intolerance only to shift decades later to the inauthentic docility of the New Age doctrine. In my case, the **deception** was even more blatant. If you're born a wolf, you can't pass yourself off as a sheep, even by painting yourself white. Today, I'm somewhere in the elastic midpoint of the two extremes of tolerance–intolerance, flexibility–rigidity and acceptance–resistance of Serginess, but not midway between the general abstract concepts.

Acceptance

Everyone is born and raised in a particular set of circumstances. My tendency toward acceptance depends on my energy or stress level and other factors, such as the climate or temperature. But in general, I let everything happen inside so I understand myself and life better. And I struggle less against the tide.

Acceptance is not a trick to restructure our thoughts, deceive our bodies and get by. It is not a stepping stone to rise above others and bask in newfound joy and optimism. Acceptance is not about smiling in the face of adversity or becoming inured to life's bitterness.

Acceptance is about following the rhythm, adapting and adjusting. It is about opening up, welcoming and receiving. It is about learning, embracing and consenting. It is about inviting, including and integrating. It is about giving up on pretending and maintaining appearances. It is about acknowledging and being humble. It is about yielding, letting go and no longer trying to fix things. It is about understanding that it wasn't a problem until you tried to solve it. It is about giving space, gaining perspective and letting yourself be for a while. It is about *emotionally defusing* and creatively throwing in the towel—this entails no longer trying to avoid the inevitable, controlling and struggling so much. It is about flexibility, tolerance and freedom. It is an understanding that soothes the heart and a feeling that transforms entrenched logic. It is an autonomous movement from the emotional to the rational, from the body to the mind and from the lower pathway to the higher pathway.

Acceptance is a lifestyle and a direction, a gradual continuous process you go about a little at a time. It's not a switch or a button, but a volume dial; it's not about pushing, but about flowing more with life. It's the practice of allowing ourselves to be, a **process** that brings us closer to patience. It's not the opposite of evolving; sometimes we need to wait to evolve, and we don't always have to try to change.

To accept is to smooth over, soften and make easier. It is to become more unified and temperate, conscious and sensitive. It is to understand that trying to change the unchangeable only produces more tension. It is to make peace with the mind and body and to connect more with life. Acceptance doesn't mean defeat, but victory. It is not cowardice, but courage. It is not weakness, but strength.

Accepting doesn't mean throwing in the towel, folding our ears back, tucking our tails between our legs and resigning ourselves to doing what we're told. It includes accepting that, for now, **there are things we still don't accept**. It means freeing the natural, instinctive and intuitive part of ourselves from blame. It is not about apathy, disinterest or disengagement, but about commitment, activism and understanding.

Acceptance can be a sudden, striking snap or a quick click, but it is more often a **long and tedious process**. Those who accept more than they resist may not smile more, but they release more tension. Accepting yourself means letting everything happen inside.

Acceptance is healing because it involves showing more kindness to yourself. It cultivates wisdom because it reflects a deep understanding of life. Like your mind and the universe, your nervous system is unfathomable and therefore beyond control.

Accepting means acknowledging and opening ourselves to the **mystery of life**. It means understanding that control is an illusion and freedom is an ambivalent feeling. Sometimes control and freedom are real and actually happen, but that doesn't always depend on us. A puppet can't move the puppet master by pulling on its own strings.

AFTER CRYING OR SHOUTING, AFTER LETTING OURSELVES EXPRESS DIFFICULT EMOTIONS, WE ARE BETTER PREPARED TO UNDERSTAND AND ACCEPT WHAT IS HAPPENING.

Catharsis and **emotional release** provide the emotional distance we need to understand ourselves and to help us get closer to accepting who we are. And we repress what we keep trying to change, unconsciously piling on more tension, frustration and suffering.

Almost nobody accepts being **highly sensitive** at first. After gradually unshouldering the deep shame and guilt with which mainstream culture burdens us, we set out on the slow and steady path of accepting who we are. We move from resistance, denial, rejection and overcompensating for our guilt and shame; to feeling our own sensitivity; to half-hearted resignation and finally to true acceptance. I can't be any different from who I am, and I didn't choose to be who I am.

Acceptance is a slow, measured and **nearly unconscious** process that begins from the lower pathway. It has nothing to do with pressing a button or experiencing any sudden transformation. It almost never works by telling yourself, "You have to accept it!" or "Just deal with it!" That sounds too much like the scolding voices of our parents, teachers and bosses—those toxic authority figures who pushed unsolicited advice they had no business giving, and couldn't lead by example.

To accept something is to stop fighting against it, to allow it and let it be. This happens in stages and interludes within the overall experience. It is easier to accept what benefits us than what works against our interests. It is easier to accept what we like than what we dislike. It is easier to accept wins than losses. It is easier to accept other people's pain than our own. It is easier to accept something that others can't see than to accept something that they can see and that embarrasses us, like physical features that undermine our social confidence and make life harder.

Somatic acceptance is real because it soothes and lightens the body. The **rational** acceptance and **radical** acceptance of spirituality can be dangerous because it is not preceded by emotional release. This tends to be a form of posturing to flaunt moral superiority.

Traumas can only be accepted through emotional work. **Spirituality** is focused on other matters, though it often meddles with everything, muddying it even further. Innate talent and emotional sensitivity are often hidden among people's traumas and emotional wounds. Though a sunny loft is more appealing than a dim basement, there is much to unpack within the darker, unexplored rooms.

Spiritual practice also enforces norms and rules, preventing people from questioning them. How can I understand what I don't question or consider? Why should I follow what I don't understand? Why should I accept what I'm forced to accept as the sole truth? Spiritual practices end up behaving like our strict parents, teachers and bosses.

Our starting point in the acceptance process also matters. I wasn't accepted by anyone: not at home, not at school and not by my group of friends. As a result, I also learned not to accept anyone. My father, teachers, bosses, classmates, friends and girlfriends tried to change me, smooth out my rough edges and fix my flaws. I tried to change them too. They persistently tried to mold me, and I was more stubborn than them. The more pressure they put on me, the more resistance I put up.

I never managed to change my father, my friends or my girlfriends. My bosses were even less receptive. And they couldn't budge me an inch from my foundations.

Acceptance is linked to **honesty** and humility. A tree will not flourish more because you water it more. It has its own schedule, rhythm and journey. Likewise, acceptance often requires **patience and time**. That is why the digital society gnaws away at its foundation and spirit.

There are issues that I find unacceptable from a civic and ethical point of view. I cannot accept that my neighbor's dog wakes me up every morning by barking. I must accept that my nervous system doesn't accept it, and I must accept it and try to improve the situation. I can talk with my neighbor, negotiate, soundproof my walls or move away. You must be able to understand when acceptance means humiliation and not accept it with total peace and trust. I am under no moral obligation to accept everything.

I don't engage in passivity, disconnection or false humility, and I don't try to please everyone. It's ironic that the society of **control** and reinvention is now trying to impose the trend of acceptance on us (which is really resignation). There are things we must learn to accept and others that are intolerable and that we can't accept, such as a screaming boss, abuses of power, bad manners, poor service in some establishments and the disrespectful use of public space.

Acceptance is understanding that the origin of most thoughts, mental images, sensations and emotions is automatic and unconscious, visceral, somatic, inherited, conditioned and biographical, though impersonal, in the sense that we lack the rational and conscious ability to hold them in our minds at that moment.

Therefore, since I haven't chosen my thoughts, one can say that they don't fully belong to me. In a way, they just happen. And when they happen, they reflect me and my circumstances. They reflect my nervous system, which doesn't belong to me so much as I belong to it. It is important to try not to take the outcome too personally. I possess the same dignity in victory as I do in defeat, though I do prefer victory and like it better.

Acceptance is an internal act. In this culture of false control and change, it is an act of rebellion, not one of submission. It is about knowing what to accept, what to try to change and what to accept if we ever expect things to change. Sometimes we accept change initially; other times, we resist it at first, then end up accepting it.

It's easier to accept something if you've tried to change it before and failed. And in order to change something, you first need to acknowledge it. **Change and acceptance** can be two steps on the same staircase. It's easier to accept something we have no control over, like the weather ("We were going to play tennis, but it's raining"), than something we think we should be able to control, like getting to work on time. What if the subway breaks down? We blame ourselves and become irate.

I can accept my boss or accept that I don't accept my boss. I can accept his anger, and mine too. I can accept the idea that I have to quit my job. Accepting something depends on each context and each situation, on each person and the moment.

Acceptance is a natural process. It's unconscious and automatic. First, I experience what I feel, letting it all happen inside. What I learn from it will emerge on its own, when the time comes—there's no need to jump to conclusions while the experience is still unfolding. Once the process is complete, I may draw the **opposite conclusion**. Otherwise, if I try to force a rational lesson from an experience, I'll only be trying to avoid its unpleasant consequences.

Sometimes, in order to accept something, we must first accept nonacceptance, which brings with it frustration, helplessness, anger and fear. After a while, we may become resigned and eventually move on to acceptance. That is the difference between feeling acceptance (allowing ourselves to go through the painful process) and forcing acceptance (rationalizing it to avoid feeling pain, our faithful teacher).

I can plant and sow, propose and suggest things. I

can't force things to change. Whether a light bulb turns on does not depend directly on my will or my direct action. My finger flips the switch, and my mind observes. In the meantime, I continue living.

At first, acceptance may **fluctuate**, as some things are simple to accept, while others take a lifetime. I may accept some things one day and want to change them the next.

In the first meditation course I took twenty years ago, the teacher said that meditation would only work if it was the first and last thing we did each day. It would only be effective if we were willing to give everything up for it. He asked us to place whatever we were willing to give up for meditation in the center of the room. One of us put their phone there, and another placed their glasses. I watched in silence. I didn't make a move to put anything down. My nervous system responded with *reactance*[1] to that subtle pressure to make a radical commitment based on blind acceptance. Radical acceptance is forced. Therefore, it is imposed because it is blind.

The more I know something and the more I engage with it, the more I **understand** it and the easier it be-

1 Reactance is a psychological response to the feeling that one's freedom is being threatened or restricted. It prompts resistance to pressure, sometimes by doing the opposite of what is demanded.

comes to accept its causes, its origin and its root. Consequently, it becomes easier for us to allow it. This applies to thoughts, to our physical traits, to others' ideology, to minorities, to majorities and to everything. The shortcut to acceptance comes at the cost of prior understanding.

Initial **resistance** also makes sense. When I accept something at first, sometimes I haven't looked into it and don't understand it. I've accepted it without getting to know it. The other person doesn't feel as connected or understood, or as deeply accepted.

ACCEPTING UNPLEASANT EMOTIONS OR SITUATIONS IS A CHALLENGE. ACCEPTING WHAT IS DIFFICULT IS A CHALLENGE.

You have to stop pretending it's not difficult and engage with it instead.

I don't like being sad either. I prefer to be happy, just as I like spring better than summer and autumn better than winter. Serginess has its own priorities. It's about **allowing** us to experience all emotional states without forcing them or dwelling on them. It's about letting them express themselves and reenacting them if necessary. It's about allowing them to serve their purpose and to deliver their message, then about letting the beat of life go on.

We don't necessarily like our organism's automatic

reactions; they're neurochemical. However, once they're activated, the best thing to do is go with the flow, learn not to swim against the physiological current and let it run its course completely.

Accepting the end of a relationship or the loss of a loved one is a **tough pill to swallow**. The nervous system shuts down and resists the news, refusing to deal with the emptiness of the new situation. **Grief** is the most important process of acceptance in life. It is a shock that we can cushion and resist, but only for so long.

Many clients in their first session with me have claimed to have forgiven their **parents**. However, when we explored deeper, their anger and frustration still burned inside. We can begin to accept the first of the great truths: Our parents have loved us very much in *their* own way and almost never in *our* own way. They have given us everything, and they have also taken everything away from us. It is a **law of nature**. In order to raise, socialize and civilize us within a culture, much of our spontaneity and potential must be restricted and punished for the common good through shame and guilt.

Saying that you have accepted something is not the same as actually accepting it. True acceptance is a feeling, not a word. Without the release of the emotional tension of annoyance, fear or shock, acceptance becomes a front, or an obligation to avoid guilt. You know it's something that should happen, but it doesn't fully come to pass because the discomfort and the memories are still too vivid. First, we allow ourselves to feel whatever we feel, just as we feel it: raw, visceral, passionate, direct and therapeutic. From there, the process of acceptance rises from the bottom up.

Today, I accept my father. I understand him and can say with total certainty that he did the best he could, considering his challenges and circumstances in life. I can say this now, in my forties, after living apart from him for twenty years, having done a great deal of emotional release therapy and extensive inner work and having limited contact with him.

My acceptance began in therapy, where I unleashed all **the rage, the thirst for revenge and the violence** I had nursed toward him. As I released my difficult emotions, a larger space for knowledge and mutual understanding gradually opened up.

After unearthing long buried trauma, **rational** understanding of facts gives us greater awareness, but it doesn't necessarily lead to **visceral** acceptance. Without emotional release, reason can hold us back even more.

The universe has no morals, and nature has no ethics. Black holes absorb and destroy stars while simultaneously allowing the creation of new ones. The sunrays that make life on Earth possible also prevent life on other planets. There are both beneficial and harmful viruses and bacteria. Every living system has a constructive principle and a destructive principle. There are no good or bad things per se; it's all a matter of degree and context.

There are earthquakes, tsunamis, typhoons and deadly eruptions in **nature**. There are unscrupulous troublemakers, thieves and criminals in **society**. A protozoan infection took Linda (my dog) when she was three, and a pulmonary bacterial infection took my grandfather when he was eighty. I mourned both losses, but I didn't get angry or blame those microorganisms.

In Hinduism, the gods Brahma, Vishnu and Shiva symbolize the full cycle of life (creation, preservation and destruction). **Death** is connected to survival. Birth, life and death, in this order—the purge is necessary. Beginning, middle and end—closure is necessary. The cycle of life is the force that keeps everything both constant and changing at the same time, the wheel turning, the world moving and evolving.

Behind every murderer, psychopath or rapist is a nervous system with its origins and its background story.

Most people who divide the world into good guys and bad guys are too lazy and fanatical to dig deeper and understand the causes.

The civil and criminal codes ensure the application of justice. Some individuals must be removed from society because their failure to obey the rules puts everyone else in danger. However, if we examine these individuals' past, we can ask if they had any alternative.

I understand the criminal's mindset and his sentence, both before committing the crime and during his time in prison. I don't condone the crime or the punishment. Both are the outcomes of unchosen misery, which is the true sentence. If I had experienced what he did, what would I have done in his place?

There are people born with a **tendency toward success** and people with a **tendency toward failure**. There are people who come from a long line of failures who will succeed and adult children of successful parents who will fail.

An influencer I met has a strong tendency toward professional success. He comes from a close-knit family who all love and respect each other. He dropped out of school, got a job in sales and was quickly promoted to commercial director. When he couldn't raise his socioeconomic status any higher, he got bored and quit. He also inherited a remarkable physique and competed in mixed martial arts in Spain. He was a Spanish and European champion until a back injury forced him to retire. Then he started a YouTube channel and opened a Facebook account, and within a couple of years, he had become a millionaire on both platforms.

He's like King Midas. There are people who seem to be lucky in almost everything they do. Others have extraordinary genetics and abilities in several areas, but don't have fate on their side. Fortunately, our YouTuber doesn't read books or write, so he won't write a book telling people that if he could do it, so can everyone else. He won't try to sell people another way to become a millionaire. He's not a model or replicable example of anything. He's a rara avis, and he doesn't even know how he's accomplished what he has. He lives in a state of wonder and is grateful.

I've also met many people who seem to have been born with everything working against them. They tend to get into trouble, suffer injuries, fall ill and constantly walk on the edge. They end up in impossible relationships, get stuck in jobs that aren't good for them, battle addictions to all kinds of substances, end valuable friendships and seem to attract injustice, abuse and humiliation wherever they go.

Keith Richards is a famous functioning former drug addict who has never set foot in a detox center. He once stayed awake for nine days in a row, and is about to turn eighty. Jeff Buckley never tried drugs and accidentally drowned in a river when he was thirty. A friend's father has been in four serious traffic accidents for speeding yet always escaped unscathed. A neighbor's son crashed his car and died instantly on the same day he got his driver's license.

Look back and think of the times that a split second or a mere snap of the fingers could have kept you from being here right now. Are you aware of the times you could have died due to a miscalculation, reckless behavior or someone else's mistake?

We are terrified of the idea that we are shaped by **great biological and cultural determinism**. We think that if we are less demanding, question our perfectionism and stop making sacrifices, we'll become lazy or lose our drive to work and to thrive. We fear that deep down inside us, there's a criminal waiting for guilt to let down its guard. If that happens, our instincts, repressed by shame, will boil to the surface, and we'll end up abusing and hurting people.

We're not aware of the **psychological tension**

created by our disproportionate feelings of guilt and shame. It probably produces latent suffering and strain that cause many of our illnesses and disorders.

Reflecting won't change what is already happening, but it is within our power to act according to our true nature. We cannot predict the future or the next step. Those who claim to know the future are merely speculating, taking advantage of suggestion and ignorance. Whoever plays God on Earth is bound to commit mischief.

Life is a journey that reveals itself as we live through it. Meaning only appears when we look back. We trust in change because it will come regardless. In the meantime, let's learn to accept what we cannot change. Let's stop tilting at windmills and become more at one with who we are.

Patience

Patience is bitter, but its fruit is sweet.

Commonly attributed to
Jean-Jacques Rousseau

I'm probably one of the most impatient people I've ever known. The conflicts I faced during my childhood, teenage years and early adulthood may have been caused by my **impatience**. I have a hypersensitive, reactive and forceful nervous system. Gifted with high verbal fluency, my sharp mind processes information quickly, and I often jump to conclusions and dismiss things swiftly and superficially.

The world always moved too slowly for me. I streaked by on jet planes while others putted along on scooters. I wanted to figure out what was about to happen in class, at home and in the street. I would hurry to guess what my teacher, my friends and my father were going to say. Everything seemed so **boring and predictable**.

Boredom was just another sign of my lack of **patience**. I finished my homework quickly, played quickly, talked quickly and walked quickly. I was kicked out of class for the first time quickly, I kissed a girl for the first time quickly, and I got drunk for the first time and threw up quickly.

Speed characterized my personality. If I could catch something on the fly, that was good. If I had to dig deep, it wasn't worth the effort, and I did it my own way. Waiting was a waste of time. I couldn't stand waiting; it pained me. No one had ever waited for me anywhere.

My role models were people in a **hurry**. My father, first and foremost, was always in a rush. He would talk quickly, think quickly, joke quickly, greet people quickly and leave quickly. He would react quickly, lose his temper quickly and lose his mind quickly.

Everything happened **quickly**. My idols and role models were also people who did things fast. Slow people bored me, and slowness weighed me down. Top speeds were best for living life to the fullest.

My **speed** was **mental, verbal and physical**. It was the best and only way to be comfortable in the world. I wanted to live fast, die young and leave a good-looking corpse. I never thought I'd make it past twenty-five.

When I was a teenager, people called me "crazy" because I reacted quickly to provocation. I even went looking for fights, butting into other people's fights that I couldn't have cared less about. With cracked lips, broken hands and black eyes, I kept my self-esteem intact.

I went from being a ticking time bomb to a freight train running off the rails, from Mr. ShortFuse to Sergi Fuss, with no transitions. At night, I would fight with everyone: punching people, slapping them, throwing stones at them and hitting them with sticks. My friends threatened to cut me off if I carried on like that.

All this urgency was my downfall. If I liked a woman, I would want to kiss her. If I kissed her, I would want to have sex with her. If I had sex with her, I would want to be her boyfriend. Then I'd get bored and look for another girl.

I got tired of everything: my teachers, my family, my friends and my house. I got tired of dressing like a stupid preppy kid, of looking like my father, of not being admired, of being feared by everyone and not being understood or loved by anyone.

I started many jobs just to quit them soon after. I studied different subjects and tried out different lines of work and gave them up right away. I quickly developed several addictions to cope with my boredom, lack of direction and sense of meaninglessness during that long period.

I got hooked on meeting women, with smooth talk and burning my money to impress them. I got hooked on going out at night, taking ecstasy and coming home the next day. I was also heavily into reading, rock music, lifting weights and studying psychology.

As if I wasn't in enough of a hurry, I got my motorcycle license at twenty-one. I started working as a delivery driver and a courier. I loved my motorcycle. It made me feel alive.

At night, I would explore the dark, hidden and dangerous corners of the lost city. I would push the accelerator to the limit, zigzagging between cars, devouring the city and the whole world in big bites. I would crash into cars, flip over, knock my helmeted head on the ground and walk away unscathed.

I was addicted to getting yelled at by strangers, to giving people a piece of my mind, to hitting drivers who deserved it over and over. I would ride the wrong way, off the pavement, even on the beach and in the woods. I would run two red lights going downhill without gas.

I felt like I could **control** time, space and life itself. I wanted to speed up the pace, the pulse and the day at my whim. On the bike, my everyday life was definitely less boring. At forty miles per hour, it was much less boring. At seventy-five miles per hour into a headwind, it was thrilling. Risk, recklessness and escape were my life philosophy.

My motorcycle symbolized **adrenaline**, adventure, possibility, hope and the illusion of control and identity. It was also the only thing I owned in my name. I could stretch the day out like a piece of chewing gum, do as many things and go to as many places as other people could in a month or even in their entire lives. I rode my bike sober, drunk, high and hungover, with music blasting from my headphones. I outran the police five times. It was the end of a great era; laws were lax in Barcelona and throughout civilization.

The most hellish part of any city is the traffic. On a motorcycle, you can cut through time and space and feel like it's the world adjusting to you, and not the other way around.

After twelve years of frantic and unbridled riding, I gradually started to use my motorcycle less frequently. I needed to **walk** again and **reconnect** with the street. I needed to feel less isolated, hysterical and alone. I needed to connect with people, at a pedestrian's more leisurely pace.

It was during my intense practice of meditation that I began to forget about the motorcycle. I noticed that I felt calmer before and after riding. And when I did get on, I felt an inner transformation that left me restless and impatient. I wanted to transfer the calmness I was gaining from meditation to other parts of life, beyond just the formal practice. I was tired of being Mr. Hyde and left my motorcycle behind.

My approach to my motorcycle had been like fast food, pursuing mindlessness, and my spiritual practice and inner expansion enticed me to savor my food more to digest it better. I continued to ride my motorcycle for several years, but I also rode a bicycle, took the bus, rode the subway and walked everywhere. I eventually decided to only ride it on the weekends.

I tried to apply the principles of **meditation** to riding my motorcycle, but there was no way it could work.

It was in the distance, in that stark contrast between walking and riding my motorcycle, that I realized the devastating effect that motorcycles have on most riders. One Sunday afternoon, I emerged from a meditation retreat feeling refreshed and simple, floating and light as if I were in another dimension.

Suddenly, I remembered I had to be somewhere and I was running late. The feeling of being in a rush canceled out what clarity I had gained. A few moments later, I was speeding toward my destination. The peaceful effects of meditation had evaporated.

What was the point of meditating if I was going to lose all the progress I had made the moment I got on my motorcycle? When the pandemic hit, I sold my motorcycle. I haven't owned one since.

Rushing is the opposite of patience. When you're in a hurry, you feel stressed, pressured and tense. You merge with the **unpleasant feeling** of the moment and lose perspective. You can no longer appreciate the nuances and details, the important aspects of life. What is true, beautiful, fair and kind fades away. Binary, black-and-white division takes hold. It's you versus them in a daily war of separation.

Rushing around is ugly. It closes us off and shuts us up within ourselves. It gives us tunnel vision, leaving no room for anything or anyone else. It builds walls inside us, and we become reactive and defensive. It prompts us to **spontaneously regress** to a past thick with hurry, greed and selfishness, as well as ecpathic[1] and antisocial individualism.

Being in a hurry yanks us out of our natural rhythms and cycles. The sun, rain, trees, birds and grass are in no rush. However, bureaucracy, traffic, offices and gyms all bristle with tension and urgency.

Everyone's own personal, inner **rhythm** is being disrespected. The same constant rhythm is imposed on us all by the mainstream flogging of mediocrity. We operate with tight schedules, full agendas and packed calendars. We squeeze two clients in the same time slot, making twice as much money in half the time. All this

1 "Ecpathic" is the adjective of "ecpathy," the English translation of the Spanish term *ecpatía* (from the Greek *ek-patheia* ["feeling outward"]), coined by Dr. José Luis González de Rivera y Revuelta in 2005, which he defines as "a voluntary mental process of actively excluding feelings, attitudes, thoughts and motivations induced by others."

puts us under strain and separates us from each other as a species.

The hurry and stress I see in other people these days upsets me. Seeing people constantly tense and rushing around makes me uncomfortable. For example, I don't like bars where everyone is in a **rush**, where the servers are running around, shouting and motioning without looking at you or listening to you. This is the **worst version** of humanity possible. I go to bars to have a drink in peace, not to be engulfed by the feeling of mainstream urgency.

I don't like it when anyone else sets the **pace** for me or when anyone's haste raises my blood pressure. It's clear to me that the more we rush around, the fewer values we have. In other words, when we're in a hurry, we're all "worse" versions of ourselves. The prison of pressure quickly divides and dehumanizes us. There is only one animal fiercer than the lion, and that is the human being in a hurry, a predator in "danger of proliferation" everywhere in the world.

Rome wasn't built in a day. Rushing around is the disease of the twenty-first century.

We were taught to be **impatient** as children. We were raised to fight for what we wanted, to be fast and efficient when studying, doing our homework and doing chores, and to make as few mistakes as possible. We were taught to be in a hurry to win and to be patient in defeat. In this way, we confused the virtue of patience with throwing in the towel.

Those who rewarded us for our haste and our pursuit of excellence, those who promoted and handed down the **culture of impatience** (parents, teachers, leaders and bosses), demand patience from us as adults. They taught us that if we wanted something, we had to fight for it, even though that very struggle was often what kept us from achieving it in the end.

Today, urgency erodes relationships and feeds addictions. It cuts time short and uses technology to accelerate unconscious **compulsive consumption**. Patience is now essential for preserving mental health.

BEING PATIENT DOESN'T MEAN MISSING YOUR TRAIN, AS MANY MORE WILL COME IN TIME, AND LEARNING TO LET THEM PASS IS CRUCIAL TO FEELING CONFIDENT.

Being patient doesn't mean being passive. I can wait for **better times** to come while I focus on other things and continue living. Being patient means allowing things to follow their rhythm: a seed turns into a plant, an idea becomes a project, fruit ripens and relationships become stable. Being patient means taking your time, learning to relax and enjoying the journey.

I can **practice** patience actively, consciously and intentionally, and I'll hardly be some conformist hippie for doing so.

Patience is the virtue by which we realize that time keeps going by, the world keeps turning and life keeps unfolding without having to force anything. By being patient, we can observe the natural rhythm of things. The scenery keeps changing, like colors in the sky or sunlight on buildings.

Patience takes us out of the **spotlight**, freeing us from excessive responsibility and lifting the weight of guilt. It reveals our role in life and shows us the true extent of our participation.

Patience reveals the different stages of every process. I write a book, send it to the publisher and **wait** for a response. I make a dinner reservation, invite a friend and **wait** for a response. I deserve a raise, send an email to my boss and **wait** for a response.

Patience shows us that on one side is the mind, with its **expectations and mental rules**, and on the other is life, with its facts and its laws of nature.

Being **patient** is knowing when to act and when to wait. It allows us to observe that we are only a small link in a large chain of interactions and transactions that connects us all.

Being patient means being aware that when you've pushed yourself to the limit, there's nothing else to do but **stop and trust** in the opportunities life presents when you open yourself to them.

Building strong friendships, finding a loving partner, finishing school, saving money, learning a trade, discovering your purpose, recovering from a physical injury, coping with grief or emotional trauma—these **important things** are hard to achieve and require a good deal of patience. You need to know when to take action and when to wait.

When you reflect back on different times you've taken a beat and let yourself process events and circumstances, you'll realize how waiting and letting time pass often is good for us. Things naturally fall into place.

Knowing how to be patient assures us that what we have achieved is rightfully ours and belongs to us organically. We haven't forced or manipulated anyone or anything. We've gotten out of the way and watched as the puzzle pieces gradually fit together.

The bone heals, the relationship gets patched up and the idea matures. All we did was wait for the right moment. We get what we get because that's just the way things are supposed to go. It's the result of waiting, or properly assessing the situation, or getting the right timing, or simply of life itself. We receive our bounty with open arms, without the pride or shame of someone who has worked tirelessly trying to achieve it.

Many of the best interactions and most important achievements in my life have happened without me forcing anything. Looking back, I can make a laundry list of coincidences, chance encounters and cases of happenstance.

I like to **downplay my importance** in the process. I think it's good to remove my "active self" from the equation and experience the power that situations have over my ideas. I like to see how the fabric of my life lies under my desires and how it is often created and recreated without me being too involved. It was just the moment. Things happened, and I became a part of them.

After I dropped out of law school, I took a gap year before I started studying psychology. A friend called me and told me to come with him to Cardiff, Wales. That year that I was about to waste in Barcelona ended up being the most momentous year of my life. Much later, I moved to California with a girlfriend I had in Barcelona. It was a dream come true.

An emotional crisis is the best time to take a vacation. It is a time for yourself, dedicated to disconnecting. You take time off from work and everyday life. You use it to take care of yourself, rest, slow down, wait, trust, let things be and reconnect with people, your friends and your family. You give yourself time and space for the stagnant waters to refresh themselves.

It is a time to reconsider your goals, values and objectives, a time of vital readjustment and **overall lightness** to rest from the theater of life.

Solitude

Solitude is where one discovers
one is not alone.

Commonly attributed to Marty Rubin

People generally fall into three categories of social behavior: those who need to be surrounded by others most of the time, those who need to be alone most of the time and those who require a mix of both.

I identify with the third group. I'm a real *social loner*. I need frequent contact with my people, but I also need breaks from socializing so I can rest, create and connect with myself.

WITHOUT SOLITUDE THERE IS NO CREATIVITY AND THEREFORE NO ART, REFLECTION OR BEAUTY.

If you consider yourself an artist, whatever your discipline may be, you'll need time alone to practice and refine your art.

People who allow themselves to be alone tend to understand themselves better and are more in **touch** with their inner world, their needs, emotions, desires and limitations.

When we're alone, we can separate outside influences from what flourishes within us. We can distinguish between what we truly desire and what mainstream culture expects of us. Therefore, until we make peace with solitude, we don't truly live **life in freedom**.

When I think of solitude, I mean a beautiful, creative and **enriching solitude**. It's the kind of solitude that melds with our **personality**, shelters us, embraces us and provides us with opportunities for growth, whether through introspection, restorative rest, emotional regulation or creative endeavors. Furthermore, solitude never misleads us with its company. It reveals exactly where we are in our personal **development**.

Unless you are distinctly introverted and reticent from birth, solitude can be somewhat uncomfortable at first. Society considers it undesirable, as people who tend toward solitude are seen as weird or emotionally standoffish.

When I was a boy, I spent a lot of time in my room reading books and listening to music. I spent almost as much time in my room as I spent eating or watching television with my family or surrounded by my classmates at school. When I was fifteen and began to have more freedom to go where I wanted, I only spent the required amount of time with my family and spent as much time as I could with my friends.

I spent the same amount of time alone in my room, despite always having had a powerful need for **social contact**. Over time, I discovered that I was most comfortable with people who were similar to me.

As my artistic vision began to take shape, I increasingly retreated into my cave. During my thirteen years of daily formal spiritual practice, solitude increasingly became my faithful friend.

I learned to recognize and respect my desired pace of social contact and my cycles of solitude. I learned to discern when my hunger for socialization turned into *hypersocialization* and when *hypersocialization* required a **break from socializing** to restore balance.

Sometimes, in an effort to avoid being alone, we end up with people who make us feel particularly lonely. This **double loneliness** traps us when we desperately flee from being alone with ourselves. We endure negative interactions, humiliation and abuse because we can't tolerate being alone and can't regulate our own nervous system.

We've continued seeing partners that weren't right for us, we've been unable to end relationships, we've interrupted our grieving process to go back to ex-partners and give it another failed try, we've continued working jobs we hated, and we've stayed beside family members who've abused us. And we did it all to avoid feeling trapped in the **cage of loneliness**, which hides the key that opens new horizons.

The therapeutic role of solitude grows if we combine it with time spent in **nature**. We can contemplate the landscape and redirect our attention outside ourselves, sit on a rock and reflect from a distance, walk in silence, exercise while being swayed by the breeze, let ourselves be inspired by fresh scents or engage directly in creative projects.

The door to an infinite world of possibilities opens when birds flutter and chirp. It's hard to feel lonely when you are surrounded by color, natural silence (free from industrial noise or shouting), order, respect, beauty and the outdoors. It's hard to feel lonely lying in the shade of a tree in seventy-degree heat, barefoot, with the soles of your feet touching the grass. It's hard to feel lonely with your body resting gently yet firmly on the ground, watching nature from below, caressed by secrecy and harmony.

What if acute anxiety and depression are both symptoms of separation, loneliness, misunderstanding, resistance and guilt? We may never really know for sure, and mainstream culture isn't particularly interested in finding out. Though we suspect that it may be true.

We come from silence, and we will return to silence. We all go from the womb to the tomb, from the cradle to the grave. In between, there is movement, creativity, unity, separation, distraction, fulfillment and a lot of noise.

It is important to reconnect with the **original silence** that whispers deep within us without self-delusion or excuses, and to trust that the place we came from is the same place we're headed.

Furthermore, if we close ourselves off to silence, we end up confusing our natural rhythm with the cultural rhythm, our personal rhythm with the collective rhythm, and we become overwhelmed and exhausted. I have my own rhythm, and there is one imposed by society. Sometimes they match up, and other times they're out of sync.

If we don't learn to listen to ourselves—in the shower, in the car, in bed, on the couch, in the woods, wherever—we miss the inspiration, signs and invitations that give our own movement meaning and direction.

When we have major doubts before making big decisions, we sit in **silence** for a while. We let our values speak to us first, then our feelings, in that order. When both align, we make the best decisions possible.

We've been taught to fill silence with music and noise. We're afraid to listen to and recognize ourselves. We're afraid of discovering that we're not as special and impressive as the social image we've created for ourselves.

We tend to **flee** from silence. It makes us dizzy, similar to the feeling we get when we stand on the top floor and look down the stairwell.

We create everyday **addictions** to escape silence: our phones, television, radio, the internet, social media, tobacco, marijuana, alcohol, food, working and exercising to excess. We prefer empty company to true solitude. These are the times we live in. We are social beings, and we belong to a culture of internal disconnection.

The soul of an era is reflected by people's **behavior** in public spaces. In Spain, where I live, this is largely dominated by music without headphones, shouting, disconnection, violations of personal space and soulless interactions. In our age of noise, speed and digital androids, a moment of silence in public is like a luxurious oasis.

Earplugs help me disconnect from the frantic pace

imposed on us and take some of my autonomy back. In airports and airplanes, in bed in any city where I spend the night, I sleep soundly and reconnect with myself with my earplugs in.

Silence is a staircase with several steps. If you take the time to ascend and descend this staircase for a while, you'll experience the **contrast** between your heartbeat and the pulse of the world. This is when you'll grasp the origin of your thoughts and realize that most of them think themselves. You'll discover how randomly your feelings ebb and flow and how your mind drifts to unfinished business. You'll suddenly become excited again about the prospect of making old dreams come true.

You can continue descending the staircase. To do this, it's a good idea to close your eyes and use the contours of your body and your breathing to guide you, like the rope a free diver uses for diving. Others want to peel back deeper **layers** of existence and let go of the rope that tethers them to their space–time reality.

You can employ different techniques to have these types of experiences, though they are not innocuous. You can get lost in a sea of sensations, get flooded with overwhelming experiences or lose your psychological bearings. **Excessive** listening and introspection give no warning; this can happen suddenly and come at a high emotional cost. What starts as a spiritual journey through the cosmos may end in a meteor shower of unresolved stressors and traumas.

Silence can be experienced alone, or it can be shared. When we speak, we are two; when we are silent and look at each other, we are **one**. We can observe, listen, write, create and read better in silence. Whoever listens to you has listened to themselves.

Music inspires, guides and motivates us. There's nothing like combining activities in silence and with music, with activities done alone and with others.

When someone shares their fragility with you, dare to listen to them and stay with them, right where they are, before you encourage them to leave their emotional place behind. Before motivating them to get away from where they are, it's better to **understand** them. Sometimes words separate us, but conscious silence **brings us closer together**.

Inspiration is a spontaneous act of association, and associating is a means of connecting. Connection gives rise to interdependence, which in turn leads to mutual support. We were taught to disconnect, yet we all yearn to feel connected.

Connecting activates the magic of natural interactions that fill life with meaning. Connecting is the solution to lifeless or excessive solitude and to loneliness, which, if left untreated, can lead to a sense of emptiness, physical illness and emotional disturbance.

We can **practice** a few minutes of solitude and silence each day, putting our phone on airplane mode for just five minutes and doing whatever our body asks of us. With practice, we can increase the time by five minutes each week. This way, going offline for longer periods of time will feel more comfortable.

If we manage our time alone and use it to get in touch with ourselves, it will go from being a burden to a **relief**, from a pit to a peak. **Managed solitude** ensures that we meet our social needs in a more balanced way. We know ourselves and enjoy the warmth of our home. Then we go out, mingle with others and feel revitalized. But we don't force ourselves to be friends with anyone who is out of step with our way of being.

Likewise, enjoying being **single** guarantees that we don't end up in relationships that are not right for us. The fear of being single is a surefire way to be unhappy in a relationship. If we don't know how to be alone, we'll depend on others to regulate us and calm us down, motivate us and give our lives meaning.

Besides, this deep **need** for social contact is visible to others and causes their interest in us to wane. As mammals, we naturally value scarcity; we place more value on what is limited in quantity or difficult to obtain. Therefore, we will attract people who are just as dependent, avoidant or anxious as we are.

Being single isn't the same as being lonely. A healthy relationship with oneself is the foundation for **healthy relationships with others**. That's why it's important to learn how to be single before having a partner. By doing so, we ensure that our relationship is an addition to our lives and does not encompass our whole lives, since we can do everything on our own, such as managing our finances, regulating our emotions and keeping house. In this way, we will act from a place of desire and values and not from a place of need and anti-values.

We should only accept people with whom we grow and learn, who inspire us, who help us create and who believe in us. We should not participate in **mainstream** romantic love, based on the drama of mutual addiction between people who cannot stand on their own two feet.

If I achieve a certain level of financial health, self-awareness and professionalism, I'll be more discerning and won't throw myself into the arms of just anyone. Not being **selective** is a sign of being deeply afraid of being alone.

Chosen solitude is healthy. Chosen singlehood effectively dismantles the webs of toxic and drama-filled mainstream romantic love that reflects today's digital consumer society.

IF WE WANT TO ENJOY RESPECTFUL FRIENDSHIPS AND RELATIONSHIPS, IT IS ESSENTIAL THAT WE MANAGE TIME AND SPACE FOR OURSELVES.

You should know how to spend quality time alone, solo travel and have your own hobbies and leisure activities.

It may sound contradictory, but when I learned to be at peace with myself, I felt more connected to everything else. And I feel and understand that everything we do to avoid being alone makes us feel even lonelier. Therefore, the inability to be single feeds back into the cycle of dramatic couples we see around us.

What we share, soothes; what we blanket with silence, rots. The truth is a shield, and secrets can grow and be harmful like tumors. Yet with the wrong people, silence can be the **cure**, and oversharing can cause us problems. It's important to be careful about whom we open up to and what part of ourselves we share.

When in doubt, we should open up if we feel safe to do so depending on the context whenever possible, and if the environment and the company are deserving of it.

Finally, it is fashionable for people to flaunt a kind of fake minimalism on social media to elevate themselves above others, creating an aura of superiority, false self-sufficiency and narcissistic independence. It's a **pretense** about having everything and needing nothing.

However, not needing anything means not needing anyone. And although you should not need anything to find true, inner happiness, feeling the need to show off your solitude on social media and brand it as minimalism is a sign of loneliness. Such people relate to their surroundings condescendingly and isolate themselves while brandishing a smile made of masking tape and cardboard.

Sensitivity

You may think I'm small, but I have
a universe inside my mind.

Yoko Ono

Sensitivity is the ability to perceive sensations through the senses and react to them. There is generally great individual **variation** in our sensory perceptions and responses. Some people are extremely sensitive to noises, lights, smells or bodily sensations. Others can't see, hear, smell or feel the difference between a cotton sweater and a wool one.

In psychology, **high sensitivity** refers to the tendency toward heightened emotionality or a strong predisposition to feel emotions; a high level of sensory awareness, or an ability to perceive internal and environmental stimuli; and a strong inclination toward deep thinking or reflecting on matters and aspects that others may overlook.

Highly sensitive people probably have more sensitive synaptic receptors (or more of them) throughout their nervous system, since visible behaviors and reactions are usually expressions of an **internal neurochemical** reaction (and vice versa).

Highly sensitive people have a lower tolerance for managing high-demand sensory stimuli. This makes them tend toward hyperactivation, or intense internal responses, and they get overwhelmed more quickly.

There is probably no such thing as high adult sensitivity without childhood **wounds**. Some argue that pain suffered during childhood predisposes people to high sensitivity. Similarly, high sensitivity can predispose people to feel acute pain in situations where others do not.

Simply by living, human beings gradually become more sensitized throughout life. As time goes on, most healthy people become more inclined to the heart, to opening themselves more to feelings, to the lower pathway and to the deepest parts of themselves.

No matter how insensitive one may be genetically, many experiences will have an impact on our emotional fabric and chip away at our nervous system.

Fears, dangers, threats, disappointments, accidents, diagnoses, goodbyes, funerals, mourning and other **universal stressors** are inevitable and inherent to human life. Being alive means being open to life's bitter moments. Living is a risky activity, and sometimes it seems like a miracle that we're alive.

There are many **elderly people** who become emotional, cry and show signs of vulnerability and affection after having seemed cold, distant and as hard as a rock earlier in life. Age returns us to the innocence of our origins, and that includes our body, emotions, feelings, dreams, hopes, spirituality, gentleness and vulnerability. Many elderly people regain the sensitivity they had as children.

People who are highly sensitive not only feel things on a deeper level, but they also feel them **sooner**. Sometimes this is a matter of **depth**, and other times it is related to speed. It can also be due to a greater degree of emotional awareness.

Insensitive people are more disconnected from their nervous system. Therefore, they often don't realize that they're feeling something, or they don't know what they're feeling or the origins of their feelings. Or perhaps they take longer to recognize their feelings, or their feelings have less of an impact. However, sensitive people filter life through their nervous system, which is closely linked to their **internal responses**. There's no other way for them to experience life.

Are we really more sensitive, or are we just more **aware** of what we feel? And isn't that evolution, the lower pathway joining with the higher pathway, inter-communicating with each other? Do sensitive people have closer (and therefore more evolved) communication with their nervous system? Does mainstream culture encourage superficiality, reward insensitivity and punish human fragility?

You can't be creative, adventurous and imaginative without also being emotionally vulnerable. Living connected to our sensitivity means experiencing both the **sweet and the bitter**. Ultimately, if you don't let yourself feel weakness, you'll never understand the true complexity of who you really are. The fear of vulnerability is the fear of experiencing the fragile nature of the human condition.

Sensitive people need to surround themselves with sensitivity to validate and support their own sensitivity. They do this to bring out the best in themselves, ignite their inner light and even enlighten others. Certain people, jobs and hobbies can help them boost their confidence in themselves and calm their nervous system.

If they don't manage their environment, they can end up feeling **guilty** and victimized for their natural tendency toward sensitivity. Then they shut down, become bitter and lose motivation. They feel disoriented, bewildered and detached. They ask themselves, "What is going on with me?" or "Why am I so weird?"

And what good is sensitivity if you don't read? If you don't paint, or learn, or write? If you don't draw, or if you don't help people? What is the point of being sensitive if your friend moves away and you don't offer to help, even though you have the time?

If you don't try to express your inner world somehow, to make your life a more beautiful experience or to inspire others with random acts of kindness, sensitivity is as useful as a lamp without a bulb or a car without gas. Don't miss opportunities to give the gift of beauty, subtlety or helpfulness.

A more sensitive world would leave no room for behaviors that gratuitously overwhelm people's nervous systems. Public spaces would be governed by good taste and harmony. Inconsiderate acts, like honking your car horn for no reason, setting off firecrackers outside designated times or blowing cigarette smoke in people's faces would be banned.

TO BE SENSITIVE IS TO FEEL AND ACKNOWLEDGE OTHERS.

In order to view sensitivity as an **advantage** rather than a liability—as a pair of wings and not as a millstone—we should accentuate its pleasant, artistic and humanistic aspects. Most importantly, we should express and share our **profound perspective** with those who value the perception of beauty.

If we shared what we feel instead of hiding our emotions, and if we learned to stand up for our sensitivity with dignity, we'd be surprised to see how people understand us more than we thought possible.

In the end, we only feel **more intensely and sooner** what nearly everyone else will eventually feel and recognize to some extent: energy, beauty, justice, connection, harmony, excitement and purity, as well as fatigue, ugliness, abuse, disconnection, absence, blockage and corruption.

Opening up when we're feeling vulnerable is a way of **working together** to create a more sensitive, honest and balanced world. The crises, dilemmas and limitations that you share with others inspire them and help them with their own. We must do this with dignity, respect and responsibility, without hiding anything relating to sensitivity or emotions.

Of course, there is also no need to suddenly reveal what has been hidden throughout all human history. It is better to share little by little, without making a grand leap from opacity to *hypertransparency*.

What we push down becomes repressed. Then we repress the same issue in others. We can only help others to the extent that we've allowed ourselves to heal. We blame them for what we haven't yet resolved within, just as others blamed us.

A sensitive person's gift lies in feeling, the lower pathway, inspiration, texture, poetry, magic, art, clairvoyance, subtlety and values. They hold the hidden treasure that is invisible to the eye but is felt with the heart. As children, we were mocked. Adults taught us to repress our sensitivity, and that ended up suffocating us. The solution is to allow ourselves to feel now what hurt us back then.

We said something beautiful, and they didn't listen. We expressed something exquisitely, and they didn't understand. We were made to feel like aliens—different, excluded and alone, as if no one else felt the same.

Without checking our inner compass, without consulting with our personalized oracle, we are ships whose sails are pushed by winds that others blow. And by following in others' wake, we end up crashing against the rocks.

To reconnect with our inner selves, we must release the tension accumulated from childhood traumas until we can settle back into ourselves and trust our body: the core of our being.

We must regain our feelings of comfort, our inner world, our protective instincts, our healthy intuition and our own movement. We must go back to trusting ourselves about what we feel, with no concern for the opinions of others who aren't experiencing the same and whose story doesn't resonate with our own.

To do this, we have to stop downplaying our feelings. We can no longer minimize what others have minimized, making us feel insecure and confused. We must open our hearts to what we feel and let ourselves feel it all. We know what we are feeling, and we must stop deceiving ourselves about where we stand. We'll see if we act or remain silent, and we'll decide if what we feel is aligned with our principles.

Strong opinions are often softened with a weak **filler phrase**, like "it's kind of silly to say this, but . . ." First, we deflate our thoughts, and then we push the truth aside. How could we not struggle to express our strong emotions in front of people if we were forbidden to cry as children? Our sense of self was wrested away from us so we could depend on someone else. When a sensitive child is hurt, their naivete turns into **suspicion**. They end up distrustful of promises, happy endings and the goodness of others. Those of us whose sensitivity was wounded as children created a mental universe as teenagers where we were the center and everyone else posed a threat to our identity.

Our nervous system becomes a **lie** detector test. Our tendency toward suspicion prompts us to probe deeper into peoples' intentions. It's hard for us to let our guard down in social situations, where we've been showered with blows for being awkward and naive.

We feel easily watched, judged and singled out. That's why we tend to withdraw, become shy and feel **socially uncomfortable**. To protect ourselves, we create a private, off-limits space where we can find respite from the melodrama of conventional life.

It can be challenging to have a sensitive nervous system in a world ruled by *replicative* people, who recreate and perpetuate a popular culture based on insensitive rhythms, habits and traditions. In a stereotypical, uniform and predictable world, the sensitive nervous system tends to lean toward boredom, disenchantment, worry and anxiety.

Sensitive people **find** that many solutions proposed by academic psychology, New Age doctrine and mainstream science can cause more problems than they solve. If we follow their prescribed methods precisely, step by step, we run the risk of becoming more overwhelmed or unbalanced.

The culture of control recommends **keeping track** of calories, weight, footsteps, hours of sleep, daily expenses, monthly savings and negative thoughts. It makes us dependent on constant counting, checking and paranoid numerology.

It literally pushes us toward *quantophrenia* (the disease of measuring) and *arithmomania* (a compulsion to count). It creates an obsession with and a feeling of being trapped in self-surveillance, as well as an illusion of self-control, which produces more tension, anxiety and frustration. It sends sufferers into a neurotic loop that turns any initial relief or comfort into yet another problem.

Journaling can help bring greater awareness to those who lack it. It can be a good starting point for those new to psychology, young people and those inclined less toward reflection and more toward *replication*.

However, if we are already naturally deep and reflective, becoming more aware of our minds will not lead us anywhere new; instead, it may actually deepen the hole by making us more aware of its depth. This will lead to a fresh bout of monitoring and futile attempts at greater self-control, which will result in more self-analysis and rumination, further raising our levels of worrying, obsession and compulsion.

We tend to bounce from professional to professional in mainstream science because they reduce what ails us to one simple diagnosis; in reality, our symptoms are much more complex and multifactorial.

Sensitive people regulate themselves best by getting out of their **heads**, rather than by exploring themselves deeper. They find relief by temporarily stepping outside themselves to connect with the world and with others. They **gently resituate** themselves through movement, nature, animals and social interaction.

Those who are highly sensitive need gentle connection, understanding and communication. High sensitivity is characterized by depth, intensity, volatility, vulnerability and overwhelming feelings. From the outset, highly sensitive people are prone to self-harm and become entangled in emotional states more easily.

They are deeply reactive to orders, condescension and abruptness, which remind them of the abuse of authority when they were children and teenagers. They idealize love. Then they disdain it. They have had intense psychological romances with people they don't even know or have never spoken to. They have experienced imaginary heartbreak and prolonged grief.

It's conflicting to need so much and to make so few **requests**, to be highly sensitive but have poor emotional communication. There are also highly sensitive people who seem to be the opposite. They build an emotional shield to protect them from the outside world.

It's important that we understand ourselves so we can recognize when to open up and when to protect ourselves. It's essential to learn to put ourselves in situations where the wind and the current are in our favor.

When I feel low on **energy**, my psychological defenses weaken, and social expectations and conventions annoy me. Something inside me dries up, and I develop a sharp, cutting and intimidating edge. I become impatient, intolerant and irritable. My nervous system expands its social buffer zone to avoid being touched and prepares for attack if necessary. Feeling weak inside makes me hard on the outside.

I have learned how my **defensive system** works. It's always on guard, protecting me, because it wants me to survive. It loves me very much, so I don't censor it. I let it express itself while I become more friendly with it.

The problem isn't feeling weak, but being afraid of feeling weak—perceiving weakness as wrong, exceptional, a flaw or a disorder. If I'm **confident** in my limitations, I don't feel insecure about them.

If you ever recognize me on the street and greet me warmly, I hope to always respond with the same degree of kindness. If I don't, please don't hold it against me. Don't take it personally. It's not about you, it's about me. I'm probably low on energy, and something inside me is **protecting** itself socially.

High sensitivity encompasses a wide **range** of personalities. Not everyone feels the same way about the same things. We are not all at the same stage of self-awareness and **personal growth**.

There are people who cry when they watch a movie and cannot understand other people's feelings. Others are sensitive to people's emotions, but not to art. There are people enormously committed to social issues (helping the underprivileged) who don't show or express their emotions. There are different types of sensitivity, such as interpersonal, intrapersonal and artistic.

It's important to distinguish several concepts that overlap or are mistakenly used interchangeably: sensitivity, empathy, emotional intelligence, social awareness and good manners.

Sensitivity means feeling deeply.

Empathy means feeling what someone else feels.

Emotional intelligence involves the ability to understand emotions while also managing your own.

Social awareness means understanding the impact that individuals have on the group.

Good manners, or otherwise being cordial, means knowing how to behave politely and respectfully when the situation calls for it.

There's little point in being sensitive if you don't uphold your **values** in social groups or are critical toward others' feelings. Someone can be sensitive, empathetic and supportive of those close to them, yet disconnected from society at large. Someone else can be sensitive, be easily overwhelmed and have difficulty self-regulating their feelings.

Someone who expresses themselves bluntly may be very sensitive, and the emotional tension they feel compels them to communicate in that way. If this behavior is constant and not circumstantial, you're probably dealing with someone with high sensitivity and low empathy and social intelligence.

It's rare to find someone who possesses all five of these **qualities** at a high level. Sensitivity is only one of five qualities, so it is not enough to befriend someone just because they're sensitive.

A sensitive nervous system may not respond as expected to mainstream culture's recommendations. Since they have a more fine-tuned perception and response mechanism, they tend to become overwhelmed easily. This is why many sensitive people are prone to hypochondria, as our inner voice wants to prevent us from suffering again.

Sometimes the recommended **dose** may work for us. At other times, the exact measurement, quantity and degree of any activity, food or medicine will be something we have to discover for ourselves. Each person will have to explore these things on their own.

This requires caution and courage. Our results can

be guidelines for others, but they can never be applied universally. It's important to test, understand and embrace both our own personal risks and boundaries, to strike the right balance that stimulates us without overwhelming us. We should open the door further when something suits us and close it when it becomes too much. We should appreciate our comfort zone, but we should also know that we must expose ourselves to unpleasant experiences to develop qualities, toughen up and grow. We must gradually increase our **tolerance** for what we dislike while respecting our boundaries. We must not use a remedy that someone has only tested on themselves, all at once.

In this way, we expand our **window of tolerance** and our ability to manage problems. For example, writing down our thoughts in a journal can be helpful if we barely have any self-awareness.

If we overdo it, we can end up ruminating pointlessly and fusing with automatic thinking. We can become confused and end up retraumatized, with more anxiety.

Even if you understand their therapeutic effect, the right amount and frequency of certain substances, situations or activities are often personal and kept private. It can feel like a Herculean journey to discover your own methods of healing, and following others' footsteps blindly on rocky terrain can result in overstimulation.

Even something as innocent as sharing our feelings

can feel like a personal epic. We know that doing so sometimes brings relief, but it can also stress us out even more by plunging us back into the intensity of the feeling. It is of paramount importance that we understand our personal **dose** depending on the moment, the situation, the company and the context.

Spiritual books and practices are not immune to the risk of **overdose**. Nothing is harmless, least of all what is promoted as a panacea. Many psychology books actually steer us down the opposite path from growth, and many spiritual practices intended to bring us quick relief only end up increasing our anxiety. Everything depends on the depth, the duration, our initial state and the context in which we engage with them. None of these individual factors is mentioned in the methods prescribed to us by self-help books that promote quick fixes to complex problems.

A few examples of practices that I've seen in fast-acting self-help books include things like meditation or the use of psychedelic substances. By trying these remedies out, we enter a mental state of acute dissolution or revelation. However, these states end up sensitizing us further, leading us to "pathological emotional contagion."

When that happens, the mind no longer distinguishes between what is its own and what belongs to others. It no longer filters, shields itself or maintains boundaries.

It is wide-open and permeable, making it easy to feel flooded and overwhelmed. Dosage is rarely discussed in spiritual practices, but it should be mandatory, since the same thing in different doses can take you to heaven or hell. And I don't mean that in a poetic way.

It's important to practice **gradual actions**: doing things bit by bit. We need to get good footing with each step we take before expanding our tolerance to chaos. The process has to be smooth and stable, with proper *hormesis*. This is the art of taking small doses, little by little.

This **rhythm** is often out of step with the beat set by mainstream culture. High sensitivity tends to lead to high saturation.

Walking on hot coals barefoot, plunging into an ice bath and attending ten-day silent retreats without prior preparation can be direct paths to retraumatization. Here, what promised to heal us ends up tearing us apart.

So before we head off to hike naked through snowy mountains to manage our spikes of anxiety, how about we end our daily shower with a five-second blast of cold water? This is about acclimating our body's response to challenges. Our body is a living thing. It needs **kindness**, understanding and support rather than sudden prodding.

Years ago, I attended a workshop in Barcelona on accelerated breathing and cold exposure. The guru leading the workshop was a foreign student in his early twenties. He boasted of being a psychology student and an expert in eliminating anxiety and stress. With his simple technique, he promised to heal every physiological and emotional ailment imaginable.

Halfway through the session, one of the attendees had a severe breakdown and went into shock. He became extremely frightened and babbled in despair. Bursting into tears, he screamed inconsolably. Eventually, he shared with us that he was undergoing psychiatric treatment for clinical depression.

The young guru, who didn't speak a word of Spanish, winked at him and handed him his business card so he could continue the breathing and ice sessions with him one-on-one. Bless the hearts of the naive and reckless youth! I felt so sorry for that man. I hoped it didn't end in another "iatro-guru-genic" mess. The road to hell is paved with good intentions.

We must defend our sensitivity. We must put disrespect in check and come to see each person's way of being as normal. We need to stop telling others, "You're a jerk," "You're lazy" and "You're a whiner." Depth, curiosity, feelings and good manners are never shortcomings.

Don't take the **mainstream bait**. Don't back down

from verbal confrontation when someone attacks your personality. The words "you're," "always" and "never" have no place in sensitive dialogue.

BEING SENSITIVE ISN'T THE SAME AS BEING VULNERABLE, BUT DENYING YOUR SENSITIVITY SURE IS.

People are sensitive simply because they feel deeply, not because they're weak. The key is not to be less vulnerable, but rather to handle yourself better when you feel vulnerable. Don't force the lower pathway. It will come naturally.

We can't make ourselves like fear, but being a little less scared is a **realistic goal**. This doesn't mean that we stop being who we are, but rather that we learn to understand ourselves and handle ourselves better during fearful times. The aim is not to remain calm during emotional hyperactivation, but rather to be more **trusting**.

The **closer** we become and the more trust we build with each other, the more sensitivity we show, chipping away at all the thick walls that once kept us apart. Together we move toward each other while remaining true to ourselves. If we show ourselves transparently to each other and share who we genuinely are, we'll feel that we're not so different after all. Deep down, there are not two of us. We are only separated by form and by degree.

Not unlike our fear of fear, we also need to unlearn our conditioned response to **sadness**. Let's stop being afraid of crying. Crying isn't about losing control; it's about losing the fear of letting go. The struggle not to cry is also a struggle against the relief that **tears** bring. There's often more drama involved in holding back tears than in letting them take us all the way.

Besides, the world doesn't end when you cry. In fact, after the tears, it starts anew. This is the purpose of sadness: to open up deeper and more honest new worlds.

Don't wipe away or dry your tears; there's nothing to hide. We don't hide our teeth when we smile, so let's not hide our tears when we cry. Don't let your tears be followed by guilt, but by understanding. Don't let your tears be followed by shame, but by a sense of liberation.

Sometimes we connect better with a loved one with whom we have unresolved problems by crying instead of talking.

I don't like it when people cry, but I do appreciate it when they cry openly, without hiding it or putting on a show. It fosters communication, builds trust and strengthens bonds. It brings us closer to finding a **solution**.

We need to stop **justifying** sensitivity. Don't apologize for getting emotional in public. Never apologize to anyone for how you feel. Being sensitive doesn't make you any better or worse, and it doesn't make you right or wrong. It doesn't give you more or fewer rights than anyone else.

All emotions have their meaning and function. We don't like **anger**, but when it's properly channeled, it allows us to address unresolved issues and make it clear where we stand. **Constant joy** is superficial, however, and those who are always laughing never go deep. People who continue to put on a joyful front and nothing else lack a critical sense and therefore often *replicate* mainstream culture.

And how about denying **fear**? That's more aversion to life.

Just because someone reacts less emotionally than someone else doesn't make them any righter or any wiser. It's simply another way of being. You're not crazy for being afraid to feel; it was scared out of us. It's normal to feel fear, but that shouldn't prevent us from gently moving toward it. Of course, we also shouldn't dwell on it any more than necessary.

Insecurity isn't about feeling fear, but rather about feeling incapable of embracing the fear we have. It's important to lose the fear of feeling uncertain, uncomfortable or afraid. We must shake off the fear of feeling and of living life as we are.

Until the twentieth century, to be gentle was to be weak. Now, in the twenty-first century, showing sensitivity is another strength. This is how the species evolves, no longer blocking the lower pathway, but including it and affording it space and importance. Life is more coherent if it's lived from the bottom up, allowing us to feel everything.

Strength is the ability to be more comfortable in weakness and engage with life without reservations.

Sensitive people tend to be more profound and intense. If they aren't distracted, they anticipate and experience things sooner. They have a nervous system that detects danger, injustice, disorder and conflict because it wants a better world. Their brain is more committed to the harmony of the environment and the species.

They must listen to how their nervous system reacts and avoid ignoring its signals, as their nervous system tells them how to innovate and improve themselves and the world around them. Since their nervous system quickly becomes overwhelmed, it expertly remembers and detects what makes certain relationships or actions unsustainable, sets boundaries, and thereby makes them last longer emotionally, socially and financially.

Sometimes, emotional management has more to do with setting boundaries and saying no at the right time than sitting in the lotus position and practicing meditation.

It's not true that sensitive people have more doubts; it's just that they are more in touch with **doubt** and are more aware of it.

By living more inwardly, we think that others do too, but that's not accurate. We need to share what we feel and need with others. By **expressing** our sensitivity, it takes on all its splendor, significance and meaning. Understanding that we have more sensitivity, we should open up and trust in it more.

No one is worse at reading other people's minds than an insensitive person.

There are songs, books, series, documentaries and podcasts that stimulate and refresh our minds. We enjoy them with our morning coffee. There are others that calm and relax us, and we prefer them at night with melatonin. Nighttime is for resting, and inspiration should come to us during the day. The sensitive nervous system needs more order. Thus it protects us, making us feel more functional and less vulnerable.

Nobody who sees me walking down the street would say I'm sensitive. My size, energy, movements, gaze, gestures and appearance all suggest otherwise. There are many people who are sensitive on the inside and appear tough on the outside. Our persona, façade, mask, defense or whatever you want to call it is just a part of us.

Both our appearance and our **essence** are the outcome of organic and automatic processes. They were developed nine months before our birth, and all this time they have been beyond our control. I feel no guilt for anything I didn't choose.

No matter how much of an impulsive and conflicted troublemaker I was as a teenager, deep down I always had the capacity for feeling and self-reflection. The difference is that I didn't know that before and mistook my resentment for insensitivity.

And no matter how much of a psychologist I am, no matter how many years I've spent studying and practicing psychology, no matter how long I've followed a formal spiritual practice, no matter how widely I've traveled and read, no matter how much awareness, information, manners and sensitivity I've developed, I'm still myself in essence and form.

I believe in peace and understanding, but I won't back down from a minor confrontation if I feel the situation calls for it and the time is right.

Not all highly sensitive people fit the description of the psychologist who coined the label *highly sensitive person*. My professional experience has shown me that there are many more highly sensitive people than meet the eye. The exaggerated actions and reactions we see in people are often due to a highly sensitive and frightened nervous system visibly compensating for what is overwhelming it within.

The more lost you feel inside, the more you need to appear composed in public.

We are **gentle** and **firm**, strong and changeable. We are part of a "new breed," and one of my first tattoos on my hand is dedicated to this concept.

We can think, speak and move quickly, speak loudly, anticipate and lead. At the same time, we can be highly sensorial, profound and emotional and tune our energy level to whatever the situation demands.

We give peace and calm when we receive it. We never turn the other cheek. When we reject peace and calm, that's twentieth-century religion and guilt acting on our behalf.

Our compass is our feeling, sensitive and intuitive beating **heart** when our nervous system is liberated from guilt and shame. This is not the heart that mainstream culture promotes in dramatic, conventional and toxic terms.

Our destiny and personal truth reside in our automatic movement. They lie in **what is** and what we did not choose, yet they beat, pulse and breathe to their own rhythm within each of us.

In general, the mainstream attitude is insensitive, while the **real** one is sensitive. They want us to be frightened *digital androids* who pretend to be happy at the same time. However, we are **emotional and changeable** beings: sometimes we are firm, and other times we are gentle.

There are people who take advantage of you when you're weak. They sink their claws in you, feigning interest while also making you feel guilty. They motivate you by making you feel small and then building you back up, and when you open your heart to them, they stab it. If you dish the same treatment back to them, they feel attacked.

There are people who tell you about their problems in an elaborate way, speaking slowly with deep feeling, going into great personal detail. They seek support and connection, building a bridge between their psyche and your own. And these same people rationalize, minimize, simplify and relativize your problems when you share them.

There are people who are highly sensitive but only regarding their own feelings, and then there are people who are highly sensitive and aware of other people's feelings. The former are emotional and sensitive in their approach to their own problems and rational and abrupt with yours. It's crucial to point out this inconsistency. Sensitivity without empathy is useless.

There are people who are openly affectionate and

sensitive toward animals, yet cold and unfriendly toward humans. These people might greet dogs on the street and ignore the humans walking them. There are people who do everything backwards socially, and then call you weird.

Humans must be taken in from a distance—we are sensitive and have **principles**. We are convinced that we're not here to hide our feelings, whatever they may be, but to experience them more naturally and with less guilt. We're a new lineage, an **unclassifiable** new breed.

After centuries of abuse and misalignment, something seems to be changing in workplace culture. Enthusiastic and motivated people in mainstream circles now say that just as the past belonged to those who were "physically strong," the future belongs to "the sensitive."

There is even talk of an emotional revolution where the pace will be set by workers' feelings. They realize that **insensitive** people take greater advantage of others.

SENSITIVE PEOPLE ARE MORE RELIABLE AND HAVE VALUES AS DEEP AS THEIR FEELINGS.

It seems that in the most materialistic era humanity has ever known, there is a window to depth and sustainability that is only within the reach of sensitive people.

Introversion

I don't hate people. I just feel better when they aren't around.

Commonly attributed to Charles Bukowski

We were raised to be extroverts. At school and in col-lege, we were packed into big classrooms alongside dozens, sometimes hundreds of other students. In the hallways, on the playground and in the cafeteria, we were surrounded by the hustle and bustle of our classmates and professors. These large spaces were filled with voices, movement, noise and smells.

We were forced to read aloud in front of the class, speak in public, write things on the chalkboard and give public presentations. We were required to work in groups and take oral exams under the watchful eyes of others.

At work, we're also often surrounded by people in a hurry, speeding along with high levels of overwhelming energy. Mainstream culture is clearly interested in us being extroverted, sociable, open and friendly.

Attitudes and behaviors oriented toward solitude, silence, withdrawal and individuality are criticized. "Has the cat got your tongue?" people ask. "You're so quiet. Are you okay?" they say. "Go outside and clear your head. Go play with your friends."

We've clearly been forced, if not coerced, to be different from who we are. We've been singled out for not wanting to do what most people are supposed to like doing. Thus, the idea has spread that being extroverted is the most natural, most proper and healthiest way to be.

However, according to statistics, up to fifty percent of the world's population identifies with the trait of introversion. Imagine the *cultural entrapment* suffered by all the people belonging to this group. Completely normal behaviors of introverted people have been labeled pathological.

Are you just as **comfortable** on your couch at home as you are walking down a crowded avenue? Do you feel just as comfortable with your friends as you do in the presence of an attractive man or woman?

For the past two years, I've given my clients a quick test for high introversion. Surprisingly, ninety-nine percent scored within the introversion–ambiversion range. Only one percent fell within the extroversion range. Why is it said that only introverts need a psychologist?

Both extroversion and introversion are **natural** personality traits. The only thing that distinguishes them is their degree of sociability, meaning whether they have a strong or limited need to socialize and interact with others. Extroverts tend to thrive in livelier situations, and introverts generally prefer quieter ones.

No single **personality** trait is better than another; they depend on each context, moment and situation. An extrovert will perform better at a crowded party, full of movement and noise. An introvert will be more effective when writing a book with a deadline looming, where great pools of solitude, silence and perseverance are required.

Extroverts tend to like people, socializing and working with others. They don't mind being the center of attention. They usually focus on the outside world they share with others. Their minds tend to be preoccupied with making social plans, undertaking projects that involve other people, dating, going out in groups and chatting with others—even strangers.

In the company of others, they forget about themselves and experience inner harmony.

Extroverts function best in groups, dealing with the public and working in sales or public relations. They may also be more likely to lie and get in traffic accidents.[1]

Introverts tend to be more reserved, solitary, analytical and reflective. They focus more on their inner world (thoughts, feelings, mental images, desires and personal plans).

They prefer quiet places with little noise and low levels of stimulation. They enjoy concentration and solitude. They tend to listen more than they talk, and they are generally more cautious. They are relaxed in their own company, which is when they reconnect and regain their emotional balance.

Both can be good **leaders**. Extroverts can obviously lead with relative ease, since they have more "expertise" in social matters. However, less is known about the leadership skills of introverts. Since they are more personal in

---

1 According to Susan Cain, the author of *Quiet: The Power of Introverts in a World That Can't Stop Talking*, introverts tend to be more cautious and less prone to such impulsive behaviors. In contrast, a study published in *Frontiers in Psychology* (G. R. T. Wright, C. J. Berry, and G. Bird, "The Relationship between Personality and the Ability to Lie," [2012]) indicates that extroverts tend to rate their ability to lie higher than introverts, and this self-perception may be related to a higher frequency of lying. Moreover, a study published in *Accident Analysis & Prevention* (P. Ulleberg and T. Rundmo, "Personality, Attitudes and Risk Perception as Predictors of Risky Driving Behaviour among Young Drivers," [2003]) found that personality factors such as sensation-seeking and aggressiveness predict aberrant driving behaviors, which in turn are related to greater involvement in traffic accidents. Along these lines, see also M. Zuckerman, *Sensation Seeking and Risky Behavior*, (American Psychological Association, 2007), and D. M. Buss and T. K. Shackelford, "Cues to Infidelity," *Personality and Social Psychology Bulletin* 23(10) (1997): 1034–1046.

their treatment of others and not impulsive, they inspire more trust in people and thus can also be great leaders.

Many class representatives in school and college, and captains in team sports, are introverts. Since they tend to be more reserved, they also deal with others in deeper, more intentional ways. Their sharp listening skills and focus in conversation also help them connect better with authority.

Many prominent and socially accomplished scientists, artists, leaders, athletes and even towering geniuses have had a profound inclination to introversion.

The importance of social media has created an epidemic of **fake extroverts**. Most people who stand out in digital environments are perceived as extroverts. We easily mistake the way someone acts and appears to be at a certain moment as indicative of their real personality, day in and day out.

We admire YouTubers, public speakers, scientists, businesspeople and artists for their work, and we are impressed when they speak calmly before large audiences. We are also drawn to them because their videos have millions of views, or their posts have tons of likes. We automatically believe they are determined, energetic and extroverted people.

In my experience, having personally known, professionally worked with and in some cases even lived with such people, most of those who stand out on social media are withdrawn and introverted up close.

Maybe that's why they are so diligent in their social media activity. It's how they connect best with people. It's their therapeutic escape from the cave, the way they compensate for the difficulties they have establishing direct human relationships.

The problem with **hiding** our introversion through social media is that society ends up associating our perceived success with extroverted traits. This reinforces the pressure we received as children and marginalizes introversion all over again, as it is perceived as a set of undesirable and dysfunctional attitudes and behaviors, while extroversion is tied to more likes and views and hearts on our socials.

In **selfie culture**, where ostentation and exaggeration reign, a video of someone silent and alone, thinking, reading, writing, resting, lying down and creating would get little attention.

All millionaire influencers and social media personalities are experts at displaying exaggeratedly uninhibited social behaviors and attitudes, which are typically associated with extroversion.

Shyness is the feeling of unease and fear that arises when speaking and interacting with others. It comes from a fear of being judged and can make social situations awkward or difficult.

Shy people tend to feel insecure in social interactions, becoming self-conscious and avoiding eye contact. They easily become overwhelmed and don't like to be the focal point of conversations. They usually don't say much until they gain trust.

In contrast, people who are socially **assertive** tend to open up more to people and try new things. Introversion is a natural way of being, but shyness is unpleasant to experience. If we cross shyness and assertiveness with introversion and extroversion, we get four ways of relating socially.

Assertive extroverts have lots of friends and are the leaders of the groups to which they belong. They have no problems relating to others. Rarely feeling insecurity, self-consciousness or social fatigue, they don't understand introverted and shy people.

Shy extroverts prefer to be with people, though they sometimes feel uncomfortable and self-conscious, especially at first. They have a strong need for social interaction, but their insecurity makes them feel awkward.

Assertive introverts prefer to reflect quietly on their own, which can lead people to consider them shy. However, they may enjoy being the center of attention one day, only to seek solitude and keep a low profile the next.

Shy introverts tend to be very lonely and have few friends. They feel highly insecure in social interactions. Their advantage is that, because they have little need for social interaction, they don't have much contact with people and avoid unnecessarily awkward situations.

Seeking social contact is valuable, though it depends on the depth and conditions of each interaction. It is essential to approach introversion and shyness with maximum understanding and respect, extending it to their motives, limitations and individual gifts.

When I was a child, people assumed I was an assertive extrovert, even though I wasn't entirely at ease in groups and would sometimes feel self-conscious and draw a blank, especially in close encounters and intimate situations. It was as if I wanted attention and **recognition**, but I was uncomfortable with it at the same time.

Over time, I discovered that I wasn't the same person socially that others thought I was and that even I had ended up believing myself to be. To realize this about myself, I first had to overcome feelings of guilt and had to stop trying to make up for my limitations and meet others' social expectations by embracing my natural way of being.

I identify as an assertive introvert, and I was surprised when I took an introversion test that categorized me as markedly **ambiverted**. This was the word I needed to assemble the puzzle pieces of my personality. Until I was twenty-two, I had always led the groups to which I belonged, and I never did anything alone.

At that age, I went to live in another country for a year. I felt physical loneliness for the first time, as well as the tension of having to make an effort and go out to meet people. It was there that I realized I felt better when I didn't belong to any closed group. I liked and felt more comfortable being a social butterfly.

I enjoyed showing up and disappearing, talking to everyone one day and nobody the next. I liked being a **fluctuating** focal point. I felt more natural and unburdened without the commitment of having to lead others or make plans for them.

Later, when I lived in California, I went back to being a **social loner**. I felt motivated to socialize with smaller groups of people, but too much contact weighed me down. It was only by leaving my neighborhood, my city, my country and my culture and moving away from my family and friends that I could acknowledge my true ambiverted essence, a middle ground based on gradualness, dosage and fluctuation.

There are days when it's really easy for me to greet people, maintain eye contact and make friends. Other days, I wake up in a state of selective silence; I avoid people's gaze and have no desire to talk to anyone. When my emotional shield goes up, it's often palpable. Sometimes I'm intense and affectionate, and other times I'm more aloof and avoidant. My **social energy** is delicate and ever-changing.

Many admire my expansive, lively and extroverted energy when I think, speak and move quickly, make jokes, look others in the eye and make things happen around me. Few understand my solitary, slow and introverted side, marked by silence and stillness, by weariness after the intense experience of social interaction and by the refuge I seek in my inner world.

Serginess can shift from a pronouncedly social state to a silent one in a split second. It can happen in the middle of giving a talk, recording a video or attending a meeting. From being the center of attention, bathed in the intense heat of others' watchful eyes, I can dart to the edge and plunge into water at the drop of a hat.

The curtain falls, and something crumbles inside. The plug is pulled, and the crowd's attention fades. I go from being a performer on stage to a spectator in the audience, from being the sun to just another satellite. It's not easy to live with such a fluctuating **level of social energy**. I know many people are like this deep down, but we've masked our natural selves. We don't want people to worry, so we bury what we feel in silence and end up reluctantly fitting in.

I wish Serginess were simpler and more predictable, easier for me and other people to manage. If it had been up to me, I would have been a clear blue summer sky every day of the year. But I can't oppose my nature. I can't help it that I'm at home in the inconsistency and the variety of autumn and spring.

Weddings are noisy, and funerals are quiet. As time goes by, we not only become more sensitive but more introverted as well.

We grew up surrounded by people at school, in college and at work, including fellow students, colleagues, acquaintances, family and friends. We change our favorite shops, bars and restaurants, move to different cities, towns and countries. Now we're approaching a slower, more sedentary and socially limited life.

Age propels us toward our essence, reminding us that the end and the beginning are connected.

Mainstream culture is slowly pushing us out of forced **hypersocialization** and pulling us inward to the comfortable realm of the sensitive and introverted. What was once a problem is ultimately the solution.

If we replaced half the smiling faces on social media with twice as many deep conversations, if introverts were encouraged and empowered by society to come out of their emotional closet and no longer felt the need to constantly have to make a case for who they truly are, maybe fewer people would feel depressed or compelled to harm themselves. Making a good impression online is overrated.

Fluctuation

For every complex problem there is an answer that is clear, simple and wrong.

Henry Louis Mencken

When I came back from California, I tattooed the motto *Intus ut libet, foris ut moris est* on my forearm. Inside I am free, but outside it depends on the circumstances. This midpoint represented me. It made me feel righteous.

With time, I came to realize that I don't feel free because I can choose to think or feel whatever I want, whenever I want, but because I don't struggle against the thoughts in my mind and the feelings in my body.

Inwardly, I **allow** myself to feel everything. Outwardly, I try to adapt to the demands of the circumstances, the situations and the events that life sends my way.

I'm a **mirror**: I give back what I receive. Sometimes I feel like a hammer, and other times, depending on the occasion, I feel like a sponge. If someone gives me affection, I give them affection back. If someone hits me, I hit them back twice. The second blow springs from fear and my sense of injustice. Some people only learn empathy from experiences, when they go through what they put you through.

In the end, I am who I am. I don't seek to rise above my circumstances or the facts. I don't want to come off as some divine figure who is above it all, moralizing down to others.

I HAVE NO INTEREST IN PRETENDING TO BE SOMEONE I'M NOT.

The truth is the straightest path, even if it can sometimes be narrow and steep.

I can be talkative or quiet, friendly or unfriendly. I can look you right in the eye, or I can avoid your gaze. I'm a **chameleon**. It all depends on what the situation calls for and on my energy level and how comfortable I feel. I have little control over any of this. I know this because I tried to assert control during thirteen years of formal spiritual practice.

Weirdness has a component of **psychological complexity**. Weird people are highly sensitive, introverted and thoughtful. And because of these traits, vilified by most, we were made to feel bad as children. People would say, "Don't be shy!", "You're too sensitive!", "You think you're so smart!" and "Don't be stupid!"

If you're sensitive, you feel ashamed for not meeting expectations and for being weak. If you're intelligent, you feel guilty for exceeding expectations and for being arrogant or having a "big ego."

It's easier to **acknowledge being sensitive** than being intelligent. In general, bowing your head and displaying false humility is more socially acceptable. Being intelligent entails the bitterness of not feeling all that smart—the discomfort that each discovery reveals new evidence and that every answer gives rise to more questions. Knowledge is so vast and time is so limited that our conscious mind's inability to process all the information overwhelms us.

I tattooed *Homo INSIPIENS* on my head to accept and be at peace with my limitations. I also wanted to make a point against the know-it-all *Homo sapiens* and acknowledge my ignorance.

For me, that means accepting the humanity of being human; *ignoramus et ignorabimus* (we do not know and we will not know) is the only demonstrable certainty, contrary to the idea of wisdom spread by the religion of mainstream science.

I believe we live off ideas, hypotheses and partial solutions constrained by **circumstances** within a specific time period. We do not handle objective, infallible truths that can be extrapolated to all contexts. Any change is inherently possible, though it does not always depend on an individual act of will.

Life, the universe and the mind are space–time phenomena so vast and **complex** that they must be considered a *mysterium tremendum*. Anyone who is not humbled and fascinated by this concept, that the universe is an enigma, hasn't understood their own curiosity.

One cannot grasp the complexities of life with intelligence alone. REAL intelligence isn't just the ability to memorize facts but the ability to question the facts we're forced to memorize.

There are things I don't have to know; I've thrown in the towel in that respect. I don't want to have all the answers, and I'm not a wise man waiting for enlightenment in my rocking chair. Still, I can't help but feel **curious** and interested in amassing a certain amount of knowledge.

When something interests us, we sit down and concentrate on it without even realizing it. It's an automatic process. We don't have to make an effort. Focus comes to us on its own.

Our **creativity** is sparked, leading to branching thoughts and compulsive associations. We are filled with the desire to learn about the thing that interests us. We want to understand it and explain it to ourselves, to others and to even more people after that.

We want to explain it in different ways and in different languages, both to delight the attentive and to awaken the distracted. We continue, absorbed, until we venture too deep and **we merge** with the intensity of the issue and with the excitement of questioning.

We lose track of time until we suddenly feel a lump in our throat and tunnel vision makes us feel claustrophobic. Then, once again, we have to rush away from what had been a comfortable island.

We can't help but be critical and rebellious nonconformists driven to excess. It's part of our nature. We can't stop being children of mainstream greed.

If you're sensitive, introverted and reflective, you probably have a *fluctuating personality*.

You wanted to go to that party but canceled at the last minute. You had just arrived at the bar, but you already longed to leave. You never wanted to come in the first place, and yet you were the last to go. We are fragile, like the wind, the tide or the temperature. And we are even more unpredictable and uncontrollable.

Internal **cycles** constantly open and close. We are displaced and repositioned with the flick of a switch. What had stopped working suddenly starts working again.

We need to pace ourselves, to take a pause on occasion in order to press on. Sometimes, we'll only be able to continue if we know we can take a break later on. Our

changing energy level depends on the environment and the situation. If we like what we're doing, our strength builds, and we focus like a laser. If we're bored, we feel listless and fatigued, and if we're not conscious of our boredom and nothing particularly bad has happened, we may catastrophize that we're too stagnant, becoming discouraged and hopeless.

Our internal states can **change** several times a day. We can feel the full range of emotions in just a few hours, and we let ourselves feel it all. We don't have just one way of doing things, and we don't have the same explanation for why we do them.

Fluctuation is the quality that allows us to survive within a largely *replicative*, predictable and monotonous culture. We go in and out, up and down, immerse ourselves and return to the surface. In this subtle and constant cascading movement, we breathe and flow better with life.

We were born with fluidity and malleability, and yet we were harshly instructed to be solid and grounded. Our story is that of an animal wounded by mistrust that must learn to trust.

We're asked to be a fixed and serious streetlamp, consistently lit, a glaring spotlight in an Olympic stadium, but we're more like starlight that flickers and blinks in the dark night. You have to be **brave** to move out of sync with mainstream culture and keep moving forward!

Inconstancy is another useful and laudable way to live. I'm not good at working in a team or taking orders. I'm not good at working under pressure or being persistent. That's honestly just how I am. And that's how we're all told we should be in an ideal world that doesn't exist.

When I was studying psychology, I barely left my room; these days, I can barely stay in the same room for a few hours without feeling claustrophobic. We're changeable, and we believe in change. It will come anyway, guaranteed, even if it doesn't depend exclusively on us.

We can't stop being who we are, even when we seem different. We're just **fluctuating**. We're artists and scientists, spiritualists and materialists, superficial and profound. One month we're convinced believers, and the next month, we're agnostics. Then the month after that, we're die-hard skeptics.

We are the hinge between opposites.

One summer, I isolated myself in a remote village in the Pyrenees to finish my PhD dissertation. It was becoming an uphill struggle. I felt drained. I was sick of working on it and felt unmotivated. However, the end was in sight, and I needed to shut myself away with no distractions so I could finally reach the finish line.

After a bus trip that lasted several hours, I arrived

at my temporary home for a week. It was the middle of August, when everyone in Spain was on vacation, lounging at the beach, attending parties and hypersocializing to the extreme. And there I was, isolated from the world—**alone** and exiled in a house that was so old that it was falling apart.

When I got to my room, I felt a charge of emotions erupt throughout my body. I felt fear, sadness, loneliness, confusion and frustration. I sat down in a chair and burst into tears, stomping on the floor to **support** my release. Twenty minutes later, I felt relieved, calm and grounded.

I spent a wonderful week in silence and in cool temperatures, surrounded by nature and just a few people.

Something similar happened last summer when I went to spend July alone in Stockholm. The flight left Barcelona in the early morning, and I had hardly slept the night before. I arrived dressed for summer, but it was cold and pouring.

I felt much like I had in the Pyrenees: confused, claustrophobic and full of regret. But despite feeling down, I decided to stick to my plan. I slept well that night, and the following day, I regained my sense of **adventure** and confidence in my decision.

Something similar has happened to me at the start of every serious, long-term relationship I've ever had. It's the same anxiety I've experienced in the past when

I've begun taking singing or guitar lessons. It's the feeling of wading into something vast with a risk of possible failure.

The first time I realized I was a slow starter—that no matter how much I love and am motivated by something, it's hard for me to get started—was in 2016, when I recorded a podcast for YouTube. In every one of the more than forty episodes I've recorded, I've had the same exact feeling: like I was losing control, I didn't know what I was doing and I was heading straight off a cliff. I felt dizzy, empty, constrained and consumed by a wavering, existential form of hyperobservation.

At first, it's hard to get into the swing of doing something new; it's as if something is holding me back. I struggle to get things **started**, and I only really start enjoying myself once I'm fully immersed in the experience. I'm aware that this often isn't observable from the outside.

Maybe it's a passive kind of rebellion against something I have to do. Maybe something inside me associates it with a form of despotic authority. "You must do it now!" Some might call it **self-sabotage**, though I know perfectly well that Serginess loves me and wants the best for me.

There are times when **nostalgia** hits, and we need to dive in to touch the reef. The depth is made of the same mystery as the beginning and the end. We need a good shock to understand what life is really about.

We need to feel moved to regain hope and meaning, touch base, return to the core and recover the foundations lost in the tedium of everyday life.

Role models **inspire** us. We listen again, reread and view their old work with fresh eyes. We've surely trod the same path. We notice new details with every reevaluation of their work, and we plumb with more depth. For a moment, we reconnect with the heroes who rescued us from so much ugliness and vulgarity. And they rescue us again. We are not alone, and we are not so mistaken.

A week before Fernando Sánchez Dragó died, I was browsing his videos on YouTube, marveling at his verbal prowess, intellectual pride and provocative, rebellious spirit.

Two days before Antonio Gala's death, I was watching videos of his epic moments on television, enchanted by his sharp sensitivity, eloquence and critical mind. I had even sent a video of him defining freedom to several friends.

These feelings washed over me when I was leaving the town I had lived in for nine months. It was time to move again, the fourth move in three years. It was a time of nostalgia, of **saying goodbye** again.

I was aware that this period of my life that was drawing to a close was actually quite dull, one that wouldn't be defined by any personal milestones. The place I was leaving wouldn't have any lasting sentimental value for me, even though it had been my home and my refuge. When I first moved there, I had believed that it could be memorable for me and that I could have created things there.

But despite all the things that don't affect us or leave a mark, the fluctuating mind is nourished on sensitivity and nostalgia. It felt good to place emphasis on this period, no matter how insignificant it might have seemed to me. Saying goodbye connects us with the end of things. The heart has its reasons that reason does not know. Such is the capricious nature of the lower pathway.

Nostalgia can blend with joy, fear and meaning. In one moment, seemingly distinct feelings overlap. Then we leap from one to the next, expanding their range. Once again, a desire blooms to resume the path toward a new adventure that fulfills our complex expectations, that perfect dose of calmness and social stimulation. We are social loners.

WE ARE COHERENT BECAUSE WE ACCEPT OUR CONTRADICTORY NATURE.

Contradiction is a normal state of mind. Thoughts are pitted against thoughts, feelings against feelings and desires against desires. And thoughts struggle against feelings, and desires clash with thoughts, fear and courage.

There is nothing more contradictory than our body–mind organism.

We are children of a **contradictory** culture and upbringing. Being coherent means embracing the contradictory nature of being human and acknowledging what is important to us. We strive to lead the life we want, despite the constant contradictions.

I'm **inspired** by seemingly contradictory concepts and stories, such as the story of a boy who hated a lot, then accepted more; a boy who was lost, then found himself; a boy who fell into a pit, managed to climb out and now helps others do the same; a weird boy who ended up helping people be more authentic; a formerly apathetic boy who is now sensitive and committed.

And yet there is also the story of a self-centered boy who realized that **connecting** with people is the true path; a boy who initially despised academic psychology, then ended up becoming a psychology professor at a university; a convinced scientist who embraced and now delights in the subtlety of the spirit.

Breaking old structures, molds, stereotypes and labels is the story of my life. For a story to be complete, it must come full circle, with the beginning and the end touching and the past and the future complementing each other. Essentially, contradiction maintains the coherence of those in the process of finding themselves.

Those who have embraced the broad range of their own possibilities, with all their corners and edges, nooks and crannies, appreciate the beauty of being **weird**. Those who are not afraid to recognize themselves as a self-conscious, wildly unrestrained spinning top appreciate the **beauty** of being weird.

Sometimes you think you've come up with a lasting solution, and you write it down on a piece of paper, put it away somewhere and forget about it. Another day you feel something in your pocket and take out a deformed and hardened object. You had put the solution in the washing machine with your pants. You continue empty-handed, *ad eternum et ad infinitum*.

José Luis Sampedro was a Spanish banker who ended up repudiating the banking system. Fernando Sánchez Dragó was a rich kid from a good family who cofounded the Communist Party of Spain. Antonio Escohotado was an antiestablishment hippie who died a neoliberal and a libertarian.

You can be sad and calm, agitated and confident at the same time. Sometimes, concern in a sign of conscience and guilt, leading to a desire to set things right.

It's hard to grow without feeling uncomfortable first. We all want to be **happy**, but the kind of happiness promoted by mainstream culture and commercialism makes people more ecpathic, superficial and self-involved.

We are ambiverts, introverts, contradictory and **ambiguous** when it comes to certain issues. Sometimes our desires conflict and our energy levels fluctuate in the span of minutes. Sometimes we are a sea of doubts, and other times we are a flashing lightning bolt in the desert night, focused, assured and steadfast in our beliefs. It's the fear that disturbs us, not the movement itself; inside there is room for everything.

A realistic goal is for me to like something more often than I dislike it. However, it's more complicated for us to fall head over heels in love with something or for something to absolutely disgust us. Sensitivity makes us **discontinuous**, and the extremes blend together in varying degrees based on our mood.

We are more connected with our body. Our organism is a living and organic container. Think of your body as the sky. The sun, the moon, clouds, rain and humidity all circulate within the great expanse of the sky, and they are constantly in motion. These celestial bodies and atmospheric phenomena are unstable and ever-changing, and this cycle of motion continues on and on.

I love talking with people, especially if they are polite, sensitive and intelligent. But in the end, I only talk to a few people regularly. I struggle to speak just to fill the silence, and small talk baffles me. I can chat with a server at a restaurant, but it takes me a bit to relax when I first join a group. I'm reserved and polite, though it can depend on the moment.

The gift of **versatility** is the gift of knowing both worlds, dreams and nightmares, glory and misery, oppressor and oppressed. Twice I intervened when I saw two strangers mistreating their partners in the street. Both women turned aggressively against me.

Victim and victimizer **coexist** in each person's internal maze. We don't know the full context or everything that happens behind the scenes before the alarm goes off and the truth is revealed.

Where is the middle ground? What if looking for balance pushes it further way? What if balance only appears when we stumble onto it? What if it dissolves when we embrace it? Eternally, we go on, constantly in motion.

We must recognize unflinchingly that we are more **difficult** than we think. We do ourselves and others a favor when we live openly, acknowledging that we are complex, unclassifiable, psychologically contradictory and consistent with our principles. We must learn not to complicate our lives unnecessarily, to be more practical and make things easier for ourselves.

There are many **reasons** behind the events that transpire in our lives. We should aim to avoid overthinking things that lack any rational, linear or simple explanation.

We must find the joy in **transitions** and midpoints: autumn, fluctuation, change, contrast, difference, "meanwhile," the journey between opposite ends. We must find meaning in organic **metamorphosis**, in being open to change.

Internal **oscillation** leads to waves of creativity, inspiring us to think through a different lens and wash away ingrained biases and prejudices.

In this uncertain world that we live in, the fluctuating personality takes the lead.

We demystify the beginning and the end, the origin and destination. We focus on the journey rather than any specific endpoint. Intellectually, emotionally and spiritually, we are never completely static. Restless and comfortable, we are forever youthful.

Quality of life is often viewed as a one-size-fits-all concept, as if the exact same formula could be applied to everyone. However, it is really more **subjective** and personal and springs from something deep within us, from our past experiences, preferences and personal desires.

Nobody can define what makes our individual lives of good quality.

For some, it's related to security. Maybe they come from socially insecure countries, and it's important that there are schools, hospitals and police stations nearby. Others need leisure, recreational and cultural activities where they can socialize and meet people. For others, quality of life is based on tranquility, parks and nature.

There are mornings when coffee cuts through your sleepiness and restores your creative spirit. And there are others when the same cup of coffee fails to give you a boost, even though you got a full night's sleep. Some days, a song can get you moving, and other days it doesn't inspire you, no matter how many times you listen to it.

"How are you today?" a barista at a café asks me. How do I respond? With something conventional? *Good.* Or *bad.* Or *I'm getting by.* Do I tell them exactly what I feel?

I feel **yellow,** though maybe I'm heading toward red. I feel kind of lazy and dull. I feel a little nostalgic and somewhat bored. Maybe it has to do with the end of one stage or the beginning of something that I can't yet make out on the horizon.

I feel **sick** of crossing paths with the same old faces, cars, streets and buildings in the last month. The monotony frustrates me and gives me the painful feeling that I'm not in the right place.

I feel like I need a good splash of beauty sleep, but not so much that I'd be overwhelmed. Maybe I need to take advantage of the holidays to write—to create, cultivate and make progress toward my goals—but inspiration hasn't come to me today. Even so, I keep writing anyway. There will be more time for editing later on.

Maybe my cellular mitochondria are on strike today. Or maybe I'm just tired from the intense heat. The Mediterranean summer is looming, with its predictable weather patterns, and Serginess doesn't tolerate extremes in temperature. Or maybe I have a mineral deficiency in my body.

"So, why don't you know what's wrong with you?" they ask me, surprised. Well, I don't really know. But it's an **"I don't know"** said with certainty, with firmness and dignity. It's an "I don't know" in capital letters, without a trace of doubt.

It's an "I don't know" said by someone who understands that the reasons for everything that happens, how we feel, our levels of energy, inspiration and motivation, our desire to do things and our ability to perceive beauty or ugliness do not depend directly on any **single** cause.

They also don't depend on any single voluntary, independent, forced or individual act. They come from a fragile, changing, variable and multifactorial conglomerate. They consist of many small bits of detail at once, like the formation of a gas cloud, a seismic movement or the failure of a kidney.

Sometimes we just need **silence** and a hug, touching the skin of a mammal. Sometimes we need more of a caress, and other times we need our muscles kneaded firmly, but gently.

Don't worry, I've learned to ask for it. You can trust me. I'll tell you how I feel and what I need. Just don't ask me exactly why. We have reflected, traveled, explored and discovered the **infinite** colors in the rainbow of existence. We contain **multitudes**, oceans, deserts and universes, all at the same time.

There are people who suffer just one existential crisis in life, and there are people who have one every decade. There are some who never suffer any crises, and for some, their entire lives are just one big existential crisis.

THE SPIRIT OF HUMANITY IS DIVERSE, COMPLEX AND DIFFERENT FOR US ALL.

Weirdness

All things excellent are as difficult as they are rare.

Baruch Spinoza

Most of my clients display the following personality traits, which mainstream science and psychology overlook as key for analyzing, explaining and resolving their various conflicts: high sensitivity, high intelligence, high awareness (of themselves, of relationships and of the effects of their actions) and a strong inclination to introversion or ambiversion. Their immediate resources provide them with little understanding and weak support of the circumstances, and mainstream culture, instant-gratification science and social media psychology chronically misunderstand them and heap blame on the individual.

Are we naturally weird, or were we taught that we were weird?

Both certainly play a part, but what does it really matter?

Is it normal to be ashamed and self-conscious? Or to be nervous and hesitant?

Is it normal to feel hot and sweaty? Or to be hungry and want to eat?

Is it normal for me to feel **weird**? To feel myself as I am?

What is normal is only what is frequent and typical in society, not what is correct or balanced. Going further, one could say that what is seen as normal would be considered weird if we allowed ourselves to be our true, authentic selves. Therefore, what is weird (or rare) should be normal. This would especially be the case if we dared to show more of who we really are and less of who we are expected to be, firmly and gently.

Personally, I think that my **weirdness** expresses the unfulfilled longings of others who feel normal because they fit in better. That said, I don't try to blame my weirdness on anyone, least of all myself. Psychopaths are not rare in corporate management positions, and in fact they can easily blend in and thrive there. They are less likely to teach kindergarten, where they would stand out and their powers of manipulation would be less useful, though they can be found there too. Weirdness is context-dependent. If all weird people were the same and they were evenly distributed, there would be nothing rare (or weird) about them.

If you are sensitive, you are changeable. Your emotional state varies from moment to moment, from one day to the next.

The first time I tried to **leave home**, I was seventeen. I was still a kid and didn't know where to go. In a fit of helplessness, I packed a gym bag and walked to the subway entrance. I didn't even have any money to take the subway. I had to slink back home with my tail between my legs.

I left home for good when I was twenty-two. I left behind a note in the kitchen, trying to be as conciliatory as possible despite the great distress I felt.

A year went by with no communication between my family and me. Finally, I invited my father and stepmother to a restaurant for dinner so we could slowly reconnect. At the table, I took the initiative, trying to explain my reasons for leaving as politely and caringly as possible.

They both looked at me in surprise, their mouths open, like someone witnessing a spaceship landing.

"This boy is really **weird**," was all my father muttered to his wife.

My attempt to reach out was met with abruptness, incomprehension and judgment. I felt cleaved away. I had let my guard down in search of **connection** and received a punch right in the gut. I had come in peace, and I felt they stabbed me. They mistook my sensitivity for weakness and took advantage of it.

On my motorcycle ride home, I remembered the times my teachers, my father, my stepmother and other adults had hurt my feelings. I thought they had mistaken my kindness for **weakness**, taken advantage of my naivete and abused their power. It took me years to regain contact.

I'm still not "the same as I ever was." I **evolve**.

Weirdness doesn't always mean that there's something lacking or scarce within you; it's also **abundant** and original. Beauty is also eccentric, just like weirdness.

We are inspired by **eccentric** people, those who break with established norms and give more flexibility to substance. Extravagance frees us from the rigid rules that constrain and suffocate us in the social theater of automatism and deception.

Eccentric people are excessive and show us that the seams of humanity stretch, lengthen and flatten. They validate the philosophy of walking off the beaten path.

They shed light on new ways of doing the same thing. They point out the circus of conformity, the tedium of waiting in line for something you don't care about and the absurdity of not being yourself.

They inspire us with their novelty, creativity, freedom, freshness, risk-taking and flexibility by doing things more in line with their hunches and less "just because."

The **extravagant** minority that remains constant, visible and committed ends up influencing the majority. They are individuals who are less ashamed to be who they are and feel less guilty about doing what they do.

Watching people break the mold, doing what is supposed to be impossible, flipping the script, challenging sacred tenets, writing their own dialogue and ditching one-size-fits-all models is like meeting people from another planet.

Salvador Dalí, Groucho Marx, Bobby Fischer, Muhammad Ali, Woody Allen, Dennis Rodman, Shaun Palmer, John Daly, Tyson Fury and many others have inspired me. They all did what others did, but in their own way, taking a daring approach to life in contrast to the monotony of a conventional existence.

Breaking out of the mainstream **mold** comes at a cost, as there's no going halfway. You either win over the crowd or face ostracism, become covered in glory or descend into madness. Often, the more weirdness we allow ourselves, the greater the freedom we feel. It's about going big or going home.

There are people who only allowed themselves to be weird when they were teenagers and in their early adulthood. Then they hid their weirdness when they squeezed into the mold of work, mortgages, marriage, parenthood and divorce—preconceived notions of what adulthood should look like. They got on the same traditional merry-go-round as their parents.

Until the twentieth century, internal differences were projected outward. Anyone who dressed strangely was strange. Such people liked uncommon art and music. They were on a particular personal journey and had an interesting story to tell.

They were different. They posed a **threat** to conformity, morality and good manners. They possessed presence with depth, representing the union of form and substance. They were a hammer striking against the mainstream glass ceiling.

Today, aesthetics is independent of **ethics**, and what we see on the outside no longer necessarily reflects what lies within. It often leads to the heart of nothingness. In the age of emptiness, there is an apparent rift of presence without depth.

It's an attempt at cosmetic provocation, like a squirt gun—the trend of lacking substance. Yet following this **trend** means being what others want us to be and not necessarily what we truly are.

In recent decades, we've gone from seeking to provoke to simply attracting attention, from writing a new play to making a scene in public. It is the age of cosmetic importance.

***Replicative* people reduce** psychological weirdness to aesthetic weirdness, though there are conventional people who dress strangely and people dressed conventionally who are real weirdos.

Whereas before weird people were outsiders, now they are insiders. Before they were the sting of a wound. Now they are the complacency of a smile. Before they displayed authentic incompleteness. Now they flaunt a feigned self-sufficiency.

Before, being weird was a personal means of **incitement**, of being admired or rejected. Weirdos went against the system. Now they work for it.

Today visual weirdness is almost the opposite of **risk** and protest. It is part of a *replicative* movement without substance, a byproduct of inner depletion and emptiness, rather than a lever to pull to access that story you were not allowed to tell, that you repressed and through which you could reach the forbidden gates of the soul.

I distrust the weirdness on Instagram, which I find publicly grating, histrionic, narcissistic and bombastic, with no sensitivity, intelligence, values, risk, personality or *evolutive* principle.

My **tattoos** are a form of personal expression and a way for me to have fun, break stereotypes, occupy common spaces and broaden horizons for other people. They are a way of proving people wrong, since I can look weird and also be responsible, polite, sensitive and aware.

I hope that my **shared** quirks and peculiarities can make yours more human. I hope that my weirdness can make yours normal and that your weirdness can make mine normal. Thank you for not pretending and for not hiding behind social conventions. Thank you for showing who you are, for existing and for inspiring me. I say this as one weirdo to another.

Sharing my weirdness can help you embrace your own. Psychologists should talk about themselves and about what makes them human, rather than just impart sterile knowledge from a manual. They should step down from their pedestal and engage therapeutically with their clients on a level playing field. We need less instruction and more understanding, less separation and more unity.

If I were eighteen now, I wouldn't get any tattoos. When *replicative* people adopt something and the counterculture becomes widespread, it loses its distinctive and provocative character, its essence and reason for existing.

I don't follow trends, and I don't follow orders for the sake of it.

What sets you apart makes people **uneasy** because they don't understand it. They censor your nonconformity to distance themselves from it because it reflects a part of themselves that they hide out of fear. They censor you because they censor themselves.

So please, for the future of the species, don't change. Your weirdness is your gift. What distinguishes you is your contribution to the group. Others take care of the rest. Your calling in life is your difference. What is different about each of us is what we contribute to the common good. It may seem strange, but don't hide it.

At first, **weirdos** feel inferior because of guilt. Later, they feel superior because of pride. Even further, they view their weirdness with more perspective, because they understand that our personality and matters of taste come from our nervous system. And I was never given the choice about Serginess.

Beauty

Everything has beauty, but
not everyone sees it.

Confucius

Beauty and sensitivity are the power outlet and the plug in the interior lighting process. The perception of **beauty** is one of the traits of high sensitivity. It is an aesthetic experience that surprises and overwhelms us, elevates us during emotional lows and reconnects us with life.

We have a more pressing emotional curve; we're more changeable and unstable. Who hasn't felt upset, then felt fresh wind in their sails after chatting with an understanding friend? Who hasn't been inspired by a purple sunset? Who hasn't been moved to tears by a movie, a song or a documentary? Who hasn't underlined a sentence in a book that helped them take a step ahead?

When I had depression, I took antidepressants for three weeks and felt even more miserable. The existential **fatigue** and mental fog that I was struggling through at the time had not lifted. To top it all off, I also felt numb, speechless and ashamed, and I was suffering from extreme erectile dysfunction. I'd been dragging myself through the world for three months, with no meaning or direction, drifting through decadent Barcelona.

I remember the moment a Dragonette song came on with my iPod on shuffle, chosen by the hand of fate. That delicate, intimate, soft feminine voice and the beat with just the right level of youthful energy resurrected a part of me that had been dead for months. I suddenly felt **uplifted**, light and fresh, with a renewed sense of purpose. That gentle impetus lasted all day. It set a change of direction and marked a turning point in my emotional recovery.

Sometimes we search doggedly for songs, passages in books, paintings, images or landscapes that saved us before when we were down. The beneficial effect of art on our emotions is proportional to our level of sensitivity. Sometimes the **restorative** effect is repeated, while other times it isn't. What happens when it isn't? Has the medicine for the soul stopped working? Is our perception of beauty no longer acting as an antidepressant?

Sometimes we try to force something that we can't control. We've used the top-down approach to relax our deep muscles and squeeze out a few drops of pleasure. If you do this, don't get frustrated by a lack of magical results. The nervous system is **complex** and whimsical because it's multifactorial. When something is fragile, trying to force it can make it even worse. If we open petals with our fingers, we break the flower.

Like suffering, joy, the sex drive, sleeping and falling in love, beauty is a **delicate experience**. It awakens autonomously from consciousness and fades in the same way. Let's not despair in the search for that magical setting, favorite passage, restorative scent or ideal temperature that will draw us out of the abyss and reconnect us with the source of life.

Aesthetic **experiences** that redeem and purify us come to us of their own accord. What is **real** marks its own rhythm and **finds** us. If we try to catch it, it vanishes, and if we rush toward it, it fades away like a mirage. The sublime is ever out of reach, chuckling at us.

I was eager to see Bosch's *The Garden of Earthly Delights* again in the Museo del Prado in Madrid. I had thoroughly enjoyed seeing it the first time and had been immensely inspired. I felt like a fire had been lit inside me. Fascinated, as if something had fallen into place, I took tons of notes for the rest of the day. That aesthetic **immersion** then spread to other situations outside the museum, as if the feeling had taken root in my nervous system. I glimpsed the beauty of small details in every corner of Madrid. The same thing happened with people; every person I interacted with after seeing the painting was like an unmined ore with a gemstone waiting inside.

My expectations of Bosch's painting were so high that absolutely nothing happened the second time I saw it.

Beauty reaches us through the ears, the tongue, the skin, the nose and the eyes. It can also appear within, in the form of a memory, an image or a conclusion.

Beauty is sudden. We don't look for it; it discovers us. We are passive subjects, and suddenly the bell of synchronicity rings. We are just passing by, and out of the blue, we stumble upon a joyful chance **encounter** or a happy coincidence.

Beauty lights a spark, triggering a current, a connection and **attunement**. This can happen from a mere glance, gesture or small action. A melody, image, scent, sound or memory can set off a sense of awe from something beautiful. It can happen in nature, among animals or with animals, in moments of humanity, sensitivity or passion.

It numbs our pain, gives us pleasure and respects us. It relieves our worries and ends feelings of separation. It fills us with hope and joy. Suddenly, there are no more questions, as we have the **answer**. For a moment, we stop wandering, daydreaming, going around in circles or focusing on trivial matters.

Then it expands us—not in breadth, but it elevates us inside. It feels like we have returned to the womb and that we belong to something greater at the same time.

Beauty is casual, spontaneous and organic. Beauty is authentic, different, rare and exceptional. It is that which didn't set out to impress, yet unwittingly ends up captivating us. Beauty is often experienced as a panacea and it is contagious. If I receive kindness, I give back kindness in return. If I receive gentleness, I give back gentleness in return. If I receive values, I give back values in return.

The experience of beauty sets off a **cascade** of chain reactions that invites us to create more beauty, more harmony, more meaning and more associations with other beautiful aspects of reality.

At first, we may feel embarrassed to get emotional or show our feelings. We're afraid of feeling out of control when it comes to our feelings because people might judge us. So we try to hide our emotions, bottling them up and then, eventually, erupting.

Once as a young boy, I was sitting in a movie theater with a friend. "Your eyes are like mirrors," he said, laughing when I began to tear up. The beautiful final soundtrack of the film had moved me. My nervous system used the cover of darkness like an escape valve to release my emotions. His offhand comment cut short my emotional experience and shamed me. We are made to feel guilty for our **instincts**.

These days, I **let myself** cry when it's time. I don't

waste time hiding anything. I don't hide when I laugh, so I shouldn't hide when I cry. The reason doesn't matter, and the emotion doesn't matter. It could be joy, sadness, beauty, sudden insight or anger. Once the **tap** is opened, I allow the water to flow, and I continue living my life. The nervous system is a miracle of emotional engineering, and I enjoy the moment. The pressure in my head rises, the temperature changes, the floodgates open and the moment bursts forth. It's life at its most vibrant, full of beauty, sliding down my cheeks to my neck. It moves from the inside outward, like everything **authentic**.

Sometimes we need to **share** an aesthetic experience. It's a transcendental discovery that we must announce, spread and convey, evangelizing it to our inner circle.

Those emails, text messages and voice notes that we were going to delete, that we weren't going to send, then end up sending anyway, are what change everything. That's exactly where the heart, the core, the essence and the beauty of our weirdness are hidden, inside the shell. But we were taught to minimize our sensitivity and to downplay what is most important.

They wounded our **innocence**, and we wrapped it in cotton to cushion it from others' judgment so it doesn't hurt so much. The things we were laughed at for as children continue to echo in our nervous system.

The world today is a stream of situations full of anti-values and selfish, ecpathic and ugly behaviors. We resist surrendering to beauty, and we don't allow ourselves to feel. However, if we let ourselves connect with beautiful and sweet feelings, something inside would gradually loosen up, and we would unlearn what we have been taught. Human beings would march renewed toward **unity**. In aesthetic emotion, we are one.

The purpose of sensitive, *evolutive*, profound, conscious, intelligent and weird people is to **create** and share beauty, to embellish life a little more through actions, objects and encounters. Whenever possible, let's leave things warmer, fairer, more generous, kinder and more orderly than we found them. Whenever I eat out for breakfast, I go where the servers are friendlier and more helpful and where they pay more attention to detail. The music is more beautiful, the volume is more pleasant and everything fits together better. There's no doubt that we start the day on a better foot when we're surrounded by beauty.

As we move through life, we create a world that invites us to connect more through **mutual inspiration**. Thus, we feel less isolated, less like victims of isolation, uncertainty and chaos. The world becomes a **shared** place where living and reconnecting are rewarding. We're in no hurry to disconnect from it, or to escape it at all costs.

Just as beauty soothes us, lifts us and fills us with meaning, **ugliness** depresses us, sinks us and increases our suffering. If you're sensitive and affected by beauty, ugliness also harms you. If you get a fever, you go to the hospital and are isolated in an industrial room. It's cold, with bright walls, and a fluorescent white light hangs from the ceiling. The atmosphere is gloomy. You get sick, and everything about your situation just gets worse. You're admitted with a physical problem, and you leave emotionally and spiritually devastated.

Most public buildings are **ugly** inside. Think of your local post office or city hall. I left college because of the design of the classrooms, the hallways and the faculty offices. The distinguished employees who worked there were soulless and hollow. Something inside me came unhinged and got my heartbeat racing. Those places hadn't had any fresh air flow through them in decades. I was aging at an alarming rate. I didn't want to end up there.

We're repelled by waiting rooms, public restrooms, service areas, unjustified tardiness, street violence, traffic jams and crowded gyms. Our perception of **anti-values** drives us to despair. We hate to encounter a lack of solidarity, selfishness, abruptness, arguments, elevated tones, abuses of power and all forms of mistreatment.

Ugliness is the opposite of beauty, even though mainstream culture sometimes tries to confuse us by conflating them. Whoever criticizes you for your emotions, sensitivity and aesthetic intelligence will call you inferior, weak, immature and unstable. They will try to shame you.

THEY DON'T UNDERSTAND THAT TRUE COURAGE IS ABOUT OPENING UP TO WHAT WE FEEL INSTEAD OF REPRESSING IT.

Reconcile your emotions with your thoughts instead of rationalizing your feelings. Discover your own principles instead of letting mainstream culture assign them to you. Most importantly, learn how to distinguish between what you can change and what you must **accept**.

My first aesthetic experience in my life came through **female** beauty. It was a journey from the superfluous to the profound, from the obvious to the intricately detailed. At first I was mesmerized by women's hair, their eyes, their lips, their teeth, their smiles, their necklines, the way they smelled and how it felt to kiss them. My tastes broadened, and I was eventually attracted to their temperaments, their different types of energy, their personalities, the timbres of their voices and their captivating gazes. Then I fell in love with their ability to care about others and be cared for, their verbal prowess and their tactful conversation.

The same thing happened to me with music and literature. Then came dogs and their expressive tails, starry skies, sunrises and sunsets. Later, I was entranced by the interior design of apartments, houses and hotel rooms that make you feel at home. Then I focused on intelligence and **excellence** in geniuses and the manners of everyday people. Eventually I gravitated to spiritual experiences, which have gradually expanded to fill every part of my life.

Beauty comes to guide us if we let it, without hesitation. It shows us the way back **home**: that timeless, warm place where truth, justice, respect, sensitivity, calmness and kindness are the cotton walls that swaddle our soul.

The beauty of difference is what **drives humanity forward**. It is what we contribute individually; others are already repeating everything else. The **friendly** weirdness that provokes, but doesn't invade, is pure generosity. Your weirdness is your value. Don't change what distinguishes you and doesn't harm you or anyone else. That is your **contribution**.